UNDER the AZURE

Poems of

FRANCIS JAMMES

Translated by
Janine Canan

Littlefox Press - Melbourne

Under the Azure

Published by Littlefox Press
PO Box 816 Kyneton Vic 3444 Australia
First edition© 2010 Janine Canan
This edition© 2015 Janine Canan
www.janinecanan.com

The original French poems reproduced from:
Francis Jammes: Oeuvre poétique complète
© 2006 Editions Atlantica and Association Francis
Jammes

The publisher and the author wish to express their
gratitude to Editions Atlantica and Association Francis
Jammes for granting translation rights into English
language for this edition of Francis Jammes's poems..

Photograph of Francis Jammes by courtesy of
Association Francis Jammes.
Cover photograph © 2010 Elodie Capin
Book design by Littlefox Press
ISBN: 978-0-9925562-2-8

FRANCIS JAMMES

Poète des Pyrénées

"Here you see me with beard and hair covered in eternal snow—descending the sacred mountain which belongs to that unbroken chain harmoniously encircling the world."

Jammes, *Remarks on Poetry*

Contents

III. The Purifying Spring

Preface

It is always with a great deal of emotion that I discover new writings about my poet grandfather, writings that often come from very far away and from new generations. If the poet lived through periods of obscurity in his own country, even in his beloved region of Béarn, his work has never ceased to attract the young and not-so-young poetry lovers beyond our borders. Many academic theses have been written throughout the world about this French poet who remained outside the schools and fashions of his time. Why this attention? Is it, as Robert Mallet saw it, because standing outside fashion, he could not become unfashionable? Is it because his poetry speaks to the Soul, as a woman admirer recently wrote to me?

I never knew my grandfather, who died a few years before I was born, but I have inherited his *esprit de famille* and his faith in the coming generations.

Francis Jammes lived a settled and contented life in the Basque Country for many years, until his children left home. His wife Ginette (my grandmother) wrote about this period in her memoirs: "Francis Jammes had found happiness; he had enjoyed a great share of life and the sweetness of a patriarchal household. But our life darkened after we were struck by several bereavements. Then his mother passed away in 1934, and a number of misfortunes that proved too heavy for our large family to bear, forced our daughters to leave us and to struggle valiantly on their own… They were admirably brave and left us without complaint, but the heart of the poet never recovered from the loss. He missed and dreamed of our young families and grandchildren."

To fill the terrible emptiness—no more laughter, no more pitter-patter of children and their numerous friends—my father, who was fifth in line, founded and edited a newsletter which he named *Le Familial*. This small periodical conveyed news of the family members, the village and the neighbours, and up-to-date accounts of the illustrious visitors who came to Eyhartzia. It included critical reviews of the latest movies screened at the local cinema, as well as news of the house pets. Even the parental moods were chronicled and ranked from 10 to 0! All those missing were expected to post their news. Twice a week every "exile," as well as family friends, received a copy of the *Familial*.

Many young poets came to pay their respects to Francis Jammes. And the Poet's faith in the young took concrete form when, on his sick bed, he dictated his final will to several of his young friends: "Do not worry about preserving my fame: this I trust to the future; you have work of your own to accomplish." "I dreamed," he told us, "that some of my young friends, to show their grief, had felled at the start of the old road to Orthez, two trees that were like a sunrise exploding. You were among them. And now it is up to you to express this poetry which I have only glimpsed" (from Jean Labbé's *Témoignages*).

I wish, with the humble literary means at my disposal, to express my gratitude to Janine Canan for having understood and perceived the man and his work as a whole. The work will never cease to reflect the entire life of the man—with its joys and its sorrows, its disappointments, and also its times of great serenity.

— Mireille Newman Jammes

Francis Jammes: Poet of the Pyrenees

One hundred years ago, in the French Pyrenees, a poet wrote lyrics of extraordinarily pure feeling. His name was Francis Jammes. His joyful, however sorrowful poems express an innocence and simplicity as natural as the song of a bird or the love of a child. "The essence of Jammism is tenderness, purity, mysticism, and a love of nature that saturates all this sweetness of feeling with the smell of the earth," Robert Mallet wrote in his biography. "With you," the poet Paul Claudel wrote to Jammes, "everything is original and virginal."

"To be true, my heart spoke like a child," Jammes said.

Against the current of sophisticated, rarefied Symbolism prevalent at the end of the nineteenth century, Jammes' seemingly simple, incantatory poetry of the heart, with its childlike expression of desire and lament, delight and praise, struck contemporary novelist André Gide as pure *audacity*. Yet even the greatest of the French symbolists, Stéphane Mallarmé, had to admire the country poet for his "delicate, tactful, naïve and unerring verse with its exquisite network of voices."

"I have loved Francis Jammes because he does not separate art from life," wrote the young writer Alain-Fournier, whose own life and art was sacrificed in World War I after the publication of his first novel, *Le Grand Meaulnes (The Lost Estate)*. Years after Jammes' death, novelist Jacques Borel called him *the poet of existence*: "an existence at once ordinary and enchanted...woven with dreams that contrast with a fresh and searing sensuality."

4

"You don't read Francis Jammes," Gide commented, "you breathe him; you inhale him. He enters through your senses like those Spanish balsams whose leaves and stems are as fragrant as their flowers.... In Jammes' work there is nothing but poetry and perfume.... Once you abandon yourself to him, you think he is the only poet there is."

Francis Jammes was born on December 2, 1868, in Tournay, a village nestled in the hundred-fifty-million-year-old Pyrenees mountain range, whose eleven-thousand-foot peaks, originally bordering a tropical land of dinosaurs, today separate France from Spain. According to the Greeks of the first millennium BCE, the Pyrenees were named after Pyrene, the fire goddess, daughter of King Bebryx. Not far from Tournay is the sacred Lourdes Grotto, where fourteen-year-old Bernadette Soubirous had her visions of a Lady in white only ten years before the poet's birth. By then, his family name—originating in the Hebrew name *Jacob* and passing through Greek as *Jakobos*, Latin as *Jacobus*, and Occitan, language of the troubadours, as *Jacmes*—had become *Jammes*.

When their son was eight years old, Francis' parents—Anna Bellot, daughter of Alpine merchants and nobility, and Louis-Victor Jammes, son of a Guadeluopian French physician—moved to Saint Palais in the Basque country where Louis-Victor had been appointed town registrar, That same year while in school, Francis received what he later described as his "initiation in Poetry":

A book lies open before me and suddenly without warning, I see and realize that the lines are alive!... And so, I received from

5

heaven this reed shrill and dull, humble and sublime, sad and joyful, sharper than the dart of a savage and sweeter than honey.

At the age of ten, Francis Jammes entered the *lycée* in Pau where he resided with his maternal grandparents. Two years later his family moved to the port city of Bordeaux where he spent his adolescence immersed in botany, Jules Verne and Baudelaire. There the young poet fell in love, failed his baccalaureate examination, and composed his fist eighty-nine poems, entitled *Moi (Me)*.

The day after Francis' twentieth birthday, his fifty-seven-year-old father who had been very ill, passed away. Anna took her two children back to the mountains of Orthez, the birthplace of their paternal grandfather who had emigrated to Guadeloupe in the Caribbean and died before Francis' birth. Anna's older child Marguerite soon married, while Francis found temporary, if unappealing work as a lawyer's clerk and continued to live with his mother—as he would for the rest of his life. In the evenings, mother and son often read Homer, Virgil, Cervantes, La Fontaine, Rousseau or Hugo. In 1891, twenty-three year old Francis published *Six Sonnets*—in fifty copies printed locally.

A few years later, with the support of several established writers—Mallarmé, Gide and Loti—Jammes' *Vers (Verses)*, a slim volume of free verse, and *Un Jour (One Day)*, a verse play describing a day in the life of a poet, were published in Paris. By then, Francis had already composed some of his loveliest and most unforgettable lyrics, poems steeped in a lush feminine imagery Claudel called "delicious and poignant." The haunting, delicately transparent "Mill in the Cold Woods"—that ends "and I will pass through those woods where/ that pale girl lifts her dress in water"—

6

describes what will eventually emerge as a typical jammesian moment of luminosity fusing woman, nature and the past. The vividly sensuous portrait "Schoolgirls"— "that beautiful girl so white./ She comes in a small carriage under the branches,/ during vacation when flowers bloom"—is even more characteristic. From this early period also comes the exquisite, well-known lyric "Clara d'Ellébeuse":

> Come, come, dear Clara d'Ellébeuse.
> Let us love again—if you exist.
> The olden garden has olden tulips.
> Come naked, oh Clara d'Ellébeuse.

Jammes' first work appeared in the eighteen-nineties at the height of the *Belle Époque*. In 1894, the same year that *Verses* was published, a small feminine face, finely sculpted from a twenty-five-thousand-year-old ivory mammoth tusk, had been unearthed near a cave at Brassempouy in the Pyrenean foothills: It was, and still is, the oldest representation of a human face in the world. On the south side of the Pyrenees in Spanish Catalonia, Picasso was painting his portraits in pink and blue; on the north side in French Catalonia, Maillol was starting to sculpt strong bronze women; while near the Mediterranean, arthritic old Renoir was absorbed in his voluptuous female bathers; and to the north, Monet was designing the sumptuous Giverny gardens he would be painting for decades.

Impressionism was in full radiance. Proust was ruminating *Remembrance of Things Past,* Bergson concocting *Creative Evolution,* and Mallarmé composing his final masterpiece, "A Roll of the Dice Will Never Abolish Chance." In Ireland the last of the Romantics, W. B. Yeats, born just three years before Jammes, was singing his sublime dreams to Maude Gonne. And from across the Atlantic, the lanky, free, open, optimistic verse of Walt Whitman was striking a deep chord on the continent. As the nineteenth century rolled into the twentieth, a brief golden era produced phenomenal creativity and innovation: the invention of the automobile, the telephone, the phonograph, the motion picture, the airplane and the subway; the birth of modern Einsteinian physics, Kochian medical microbiology, Freudian psychology and Picassoan art—even the Norwegian Nobel Prize. The French Empire had attained its greatest expansion.

In 1895 Jammes, now twenty-six, experienced an epiphany:

> It was during the month of April, 1895, that I was invaded—I can find no other word to express my meaning. A simultaneous explosion of all my lyrical powers took place within me. I do not know why I did not die from the blast of that violent wing striking me—that gave birth to my poem "Un Jour."

The young man journeyed to Paris where he met a group of artists that included the painter Eugène Carrière. The next year he traveled to Algeria to join the novelist André Gide. Around that time, Jammes fell in love with a young Jewish woman whom he addressed as Mamore in his "Seventh Elegy." "Tell me, tell me," he pleads, "will I be cured of what is in my heart?" And she replies, "Beloved, the snow cannot be cured of its whiteness." In "The End," Mamore becomes the Amaryllia who walks at his side, bitterly observing "the little rich girls." After two years, perhaps for his mother's sake, Francis ended their relationship.

8

In 1897 Jammes published his *Manifesto de Jammisme* that proclaims the hedgerows his school, the fields and flowers his academy. "Truth," he states, "is praise of God." His first major collection, *De l'Angélus de l'aube à l'Angélus du soir (From the Morning to the Evening Angelus)* was published by Mercure de France in 1898. A generous gathering of freely rhymed lyrics on love and nature, full of compassion for the poor and reverence for natural beauty, *Angélus* embodies the force of youthful desire, and the power of imagination to overcome separation, loss and loneliness. The book opens with an epigraph, eventually set to music by Arthur Honegger, announcing the poet's call to his "*métier sacré*":

> Among men, I was called by You, my God, and here I am who suffer and love. I speak with the voice You have given me, and I write with the words You have taught my parents, who taught me. Like a donkey I walk down the road with my head lowered, laden with bundles, making the children laugh, ready to go whenever and wherever You wish.

From the Morning to the Evening Angelus brought the poet both controversy and wide acclaim.

In the years that followed, Jammes traveled to Provence, the Alps, Holland, and Belgium where he joined "Poets against Literature." In Paris he met the religious poet Paul Claudel—younger brother of sculptor Camille Claudel—who would become instrumental in a turn toward Catholicism. In 1901 Jammes published *Le Deuil des primevères (Mourning Primroses)*, a collection of elegies and prayers balanced on the transparent line dividing poetry and prose, composed in the throes of a depression over his

9

failure to secure a lasting love relationship. His darkly ironic "Prayer to Love Sorrow" conveys the depth of his suffering:

> Oh my Sorrow, you are better than a beloved!
> For I know, when I draw my last breath,
> wrapped in my sheets, you will be there—
> Sorrow, still trying to invade my heart.

In this state, Jammes experienced a religious illumination and in 1905—the year that France, seized by anti-clerical sentiment, passed the Law of Separation of Church and State—the poet "returned" to the Catholic Church. Until then, he had seen himself as a life-affirming pagan:

> I was christened a Catholic, but that was as far as my catholicism went, that and my sympathies for its beautiful literary themes... I was a pagan, a veritable faun. Flowers, woods, women—I was in love with all that lived! ... Before I experienced Grace, there were trials, and there was Claudel....

His next work, *Clairières dans le ciel (Clearings in the Sky)*, published in 1906, revealed a marked shift toward a more religious vision, as Jammes attempted to integrate his new Catholicism with his old love of Nature. *Clearings in the Sky* culminates in a 38-part "Church Cloaked in Leaves," which in turn climaxes in the profoundly beautiful and moving "Rosary." This unique, quasi-pagan, quasi-Catholic chant was a marvel to Gide, Claudel and other contemporaries. Half a century later, the popular song-writer Georges Brassens would create, from five of its stanzas, his much-loved "Prayer." My own version, "Hail Mary," includes all fifteen devotions.

In 1907 Jammes published his *Souvenirs d'enfance* (*Memories of Childhood*), seventeen charming, sometimes ironic, sketches of a country childhood now reviewed from an expanding spiritual perspective. "Mon coeur, mon coeur," he cries in one poem; "mon coeur, mon coeur, ô mon coeur!" in another of these outpourings of the heart. These *Souvenirs* are Francis Jammes' "songs of innocence." They reflect, as do other poems of his, the tender religious iconography that developed in France during the two millennia following Jesus' crucifixion in Jerusalem, despite the harsher aspects of a Christian Church that sanctioned crusades, wars and the burning of women. As in other French art, archetypal images of a powerful Father, compassionate Mother, innocent Child and suffering Savior, are here steeped in the much, much older Nature and Goddess lore of neolithic and paleolithic Old Europe. To this ancient, indigenous, matriarchal apprehension of life Jammes, however Christian, remains faithful.

Later that year, at the advancing age of thirty-eight, Francis Jammes married a twenty-four-year-old literary admirer by the name of Geneviève ("Ginette") Goedorp. Engaged at Lourdes, the couple was wed in Bucy-le-Long, his fiancée's hometown, and settled in the town of Orthez. Madame Jammes soon gave birth to a daughter who was christened Bernadette. Six more children followed: Emmanuèle, Marie, Paul, Michel, Anne, and Françoise (who would become Sister Marie-Maïtena).

In 1912 Jammes published his prize-winning *Géorgiques chrétiennes (Christian Pastorals)*. His play *La Brebis égarée (The Lost Lamb)* was set to music by Darius Milhaud, who during his lifetime would compose dozens of vocal works based on Jammes' poetry. In Paris, the poet was introduced to Anna de Noailles whose literary salon was attended by such luminaries as Paul Claudel, Jean Cocteau, Colette, Léon Daudet (son of Alphonse), André Gide, Max Jacob, Pierre Loti, Frédéric Mistral, and Paul Valéry. When Proust's *Swann's Way* appeared in 1913, Jammes sent his praises to the author he considered "the equal of Shakespeare and Balzac." The admiration was mutual. Proust was enchanted by Jammes' impressionistic imagery—"a sincerity and clarity of vision that could disentangle and evaluate the exact sensation, the precise nuance affecting him"—and saw the poet as one of the greats.

In 1914 Germany declared war against France, and Jammes, now in his mid-forties, was appointed ambulance administrator for Orthez. Deeply saddened by the loss of many friends, he nevertheless continued to write, publishing *Cinq Prières pour le Temps de la Guerre (Five Prayers in Time of War)* and *Le Rosaire au Soleil (Rosary in the Sun)*. A part of his cycle *Tristesses (Sorrows)* was now set to music by the composer Lili Boulanger, under the title *Clairières dans le ciel*.

In 1917 Jammes received the French Academy's *Grand Prix de littérature*. And in 1918 he finally met Marcel Proust—at a reception in the home of Madame Alphonse Daudet where Milhaud's musical renditions of Claudel and Jammes were performed. A few years later Proust, from his deathbed, would ask Jammes to pray for him, for "a death sweeter than my life has been." In 1919 Jammes' *The Virgin and the Sonnets* appeared.

In spite of the *Grand Prix de littérature*, Francis Jammes never became a member of the Académie Française: his candidature was refused in 1920 and again in 1924. In 1921 the poet moved to a house in Hasparren, in the lower Basque Pyrenees, bequeathed to him by an unknown woman at the suggestion of a priest. There he wrote his three-volume *Memoirs*—which was followed by a fourth volume years later, after his death. That same year, Gide wrote in his *Journal*:

> There are certain poets, of whom Jammes is perhaps the only one among us today, who, it seems, would have written their work just the same in whatever period they had been born.... I hope for the honor of France that he could only have been born a Frenchman—but all the same I can see him writing his *Elégies* at Tibur under Augustus, his *Jean de Noarrieu* anywhere wherever; he has a very definite local flavor, it is true, but in China he would have had a Chinese flavor.... His spirit is the spirit of Jammes, not of Orthez....

In 1926 Jammes was awarded but turned down the *Légion d'Honneur,* saying that although he appreciated this attempt to compensate for the Academy's refusal, "a poet's work needs no official sanction, and the love the poet brings to it, and receives in exchange, surpasses all other rewards." That same year, Jammes published *Ma France Poétique (My Poetic France)*. In "The Poet's Prayer," Jammes asks to be filled "like a large glass painted with insects and flowers/...with the waters of candor/ that flow down the mountain to the foothills...." Over the decades many pilgrims—Francois Mauriac, Darius Milhaud, Alain-Fournier, Anna de Noailles, Saint-John Perse, as well as many lesser known admirers—traveled to the Pyrenees to taste that pure mountain water. In 1928 master poet and philosopher Paul Valéry came to pay his homage as well.

Jammes was sixty-six years old when his mother

passed away in 1934. In the following year he wrote *From Always to Forever* (*De Tout Temps à Jamais*) and *Springs (Sources)*, ten decasyllabic, ten-line poems in honor of ten sacred springs. These were the last poems to be published during his lifetime. *Springs* ends with:

> One lovely noon, when my soul flies away
> to God and the angelus sets loose its petals
> clear and blue as a lilac—may a vapor—
> a faint incense—rise from you,
> oh my spring of Ursuya,
> and follow the breeze to the house
> of my birth, dropping its fresh voice
> in rain on my roof—accompanying
> for one earthly moment—to heaven—
> my song celebrating you.

Springs was followed by *Cinq Idylles* (*Five Idylls*) and *Feux (Fires)*, final paeans to Life grounded in the elements of the earth, poems that would not be published until after his death.

By now a figure of fond reverence for the younger generation, Jammes was awarded the Academy's *Prix d'Aumale* in 1936, and spoke at the Théâtre Champs-Elysées the following year. He had followed the path of "eternal Poetry"; he had sought to affirm "simple Being"; he had not sacrificed feeling to form, which he believed should be transparent enough to dissolve into the Light.

On November 1, 1938, death pounced as Jammes had predicted: "like a young hawk on a hare blanched by many winters." The sixty-nine-year-old poet, sick with colon cancer, said to Jean Labbé, the young friend who brought him water from the Ursuya spring: "I no longer need to pray, my suffering is a prayer. I offer it entirely to

God, the rest belongs to humanity." Francis Jammes passed away on All Saints Day at his home Eyhartzia in the Pyrenees, leaving over a hundred books containing nearly eight hundred poems, twelve novellas, four volumes of memoirs and several verse plays; a correspondence with many notable French authors of his day, including Colette, Claudel, Remy de Gourmont, Anna de Noailles, Gide, Mallarmé, Mauriac, and Saint-John Perse; as well as a significant influence on contemporary writers abroad, including Jiménez and Unamuno in Spain, Rilke in Austro-Hungary, and Amy Lowell and Rexroth in the United States of America.

Twenty-five years after Francis Jammes' death, at Stanford University in California, Professor Raymond Giraud introduced his Twentieth Century French Poetry class to Jammes' unique poetry. As a nineteen-year-old French major, I was present. A few years later in 1967, Unicorn Press in Santa Barbara released a slim booklet entitled *Jammes,* containing twelve poems translated in rhyme by Teo Savory. And in the nineteen-seventies, I—by then a psychiatric resident who had published a book of poems— rediscovered the French poet in Bettina Dickie and Barry Gifford's touching translation of *Selected Poems of Francis Jammes*, published by Utah State University Press.

After the passage of two more decades and the publication of several more books of my own, I felt moved to translate a couple of Jammes' laments from *Mourning Primroses* for my 2000 poetry collection, *Changing Woman*. As I experienced the poet's gentle influence showering my own writing, I recalled the great lyricist Kenneth Rexroth's remark that Jammes may be one of the most important unrecognized influences on twentieth century American poetry. And late one night in the beginning of the twenty-first century, I found myself prowling the bookstores of the Place Saint Germain in Paris, gathering volumes of Francis Jammes for a new translation.

Over the years, along with my own writing, I had been episodically engaged in translating the work of another, equally unique poet by the name of Else Lasker-Schüler—uncannily born in the same year as Jammes. The Jewish Rhinelander and the Catholic Pyrenean naturally generated different imagery—hers more of the imagination, his more of the earth. But both loved the color blue, symbolic of pure Being. And their work shared a simplicity and purity, romanticism, mysticism and spiritual devotion—*bhakti* the Indians call it—that is rare. To convey such pure feeling has been the challenge and the joy of translating both poets, the work of translation giving me the opportunity to immerse myself more deeply and thoroughly than I would have otherwise: to savor each poem word by word, to descend into it, swim in it, love and even hate and finally transcend it. For in order to translate a poem, the translator must first enter the poem and inhabit it as if it had grown from her own experience: only this makes possible the alchemical transformation of literal words into poetry.

In *Under the Azure: Poems of Francis Jammes,* I have gathered some of Jammes' most beautiful and moving poems, the majority never before translated. The selection, in three parts, is meant to reveal both the poet's range and evolution. "When the Flowers Bloom" presents the fresh and romantic songs of innocence of Jammes' youth; "Prayer to Love Sorrow" the psychologically more complex, often longer poems of his Dark Night; and "The Purifying

16

Spring" the deceptively simple, highly condensed, masterful poems of his maturity. With this collection I hope to bring to the global English-reading public the purity, intimacy, sincerity and compassion that Jammes miraculously conveyed a hundred years ago in his native French tongue, in a voice at once contemplative and heartfelt.

In this translation I have not attempted to reproduce Jammes' customary end-rhyme, which he called "vers faux" because they were not classically rhymed, unless such a rhyme sounded natural. Instead, I have tried to echo his music in a freer and less formal way—as well as I could, given that English has such a different, frequently less musical and gracious sound effect from the French. Where poems are part of a numbered series and without title, and often when Jammes uses the first line as title, I have created titles analogous to the ones Jammes usually gave his shorter poems.

The final translations, it must be mentioned, were influenced in important ways by the knowledgeable, perceptive and inspiring observations of Australia's Littlefox publisher and editor Christine Mathieu, a well known author and anthropologist in her own right. From the beginning—when my friend Christine, who had grown up in France, learned of my translation and expressed her desire to publish it—the work became a collaboration. Carefully reading every poem, addressing issues both cultural and linguistic, she offered insights that were often transformative. I—as well as the reader—owe her our gratitude not only for her tireless assistance with countless editorial details, but above all her unambivalent support for the publication of a first major translation into English of one of France's purest poets.

Jammes' whole work can be seen as a rosary of devotion to Woman, to Nature, to God, and above all to

Love. Whatever his subject, Jammes attends with a purity, simplicity and integrity of spirit that allows him to commune directly with the very essence and power of Life. This is something precious and well worth preserving, I believe. Amid the sometime pleasures and gains of the technological revolution, our lives today have become increasingly frenetic, materialistic and mechanical. Amid patriarchy's incessant wars, continuing abuse of women, relentless devastation of human cultures and, indeed, the very Earth on which we live—humanity is undergoing the horrifying destruction of innocence itself. We dwell in a realm of increasingly dissociated sensation, unfeeling intellect, and isolated egos.

But Francis Jammes dwelled deep in the Land of Feeling. He sang for something higher and sweeter, and morally deeper. His poetry—earthy as slugs, lofty as the highest mountain peaks—never fails to show us "the beauty God gives to ordinary life" ("First Song," *Christian Georgics*). Devotee of earth, sky, water and fire; friend to shepherd and beggar, old people and young girls; lover of plants, animals, insects and so-called inanimate things—Jammes worshipped God in Life. He conversed with radiant furniture and felt the waterfalls in his own soul. "Oh, the country of my birth," he exclaims in an elegy, "how transparent it was!" And in "The Church Cloaked in Leaves": "Now...I know that each thing carries within its own Mystery."

The poet of an ever fresh innocence; a seer who saw the numinous everywhere he looked; a magician who dematerialized himself in the inner life of the world—Jammes has left us these gifts of a bygone era haunted by the eternal. May this soulful poet of the Pyrenees—who still breathes, sighs, weeps and wonders in his poems—open our

18

hearts to a more expansive, sensitive and truer vision of Life.

—Janine Canan

C'est toi la langue, ô poésie,
que tout le monde ici-bas peut comprendre.

Poetry, you are the language
everyone down here can understand.

— Francis Jammes

I. When the Flowers Bloom

J'allais dans le verger

J'allais dans le verger où les framboises au soleil
chantent sous l'azur à cause des mouches à miel.
C'est d'un âge très jeune que je vous parle.
Près des montagnes je suis né, près des montagnes.
Et je sens bien maintenant que dans mon âme
il y a de la neige, des torrents couleur de givre
et de grands pics cassés où il y a des oiseaux
de proie qui planent dans un air qui rend ivre,
et un vent qui fouette les neiges et les eaux.

Oui, je sens bien que je suis comme les montagnes.
Ma tristesse a la couleur des gentianes qui y croissent.
Je dus avoir, dans ma famille, des herborisateurs
naïfs, avec des boîtes couleur d'insecte vert,
qui, par les après-midi d'horrible chaleur,
s'enfonçaient dans l'ombre glacée des forêts,
à la recherche d'échantillons précieux
qu'ils n'eussent point échangés pour les vieux
trésors des magiciens des Bagdads merveilleuses
où les jets d'eau ont des fraîcheurs endormeuses.
Mon amour a la tendresse d'un arc-en-ciel
après une pluie d'avril où chante le soleil.
Pourquoi ai-je l'existence que j'ai? N'étais-je fait
pour vivre sur les sommets, dans l'éparpillement
de neige des troupeaux, avec un haut bâton,
à l'heure où on est grandi par la paix du jour qui tombe?

Walk in the Orchard

When I was very young
I would walk in the orchard
where raspberries buzz with honeybees
in the sunshine under azure skies.
I was born near the mountains — the mountains!
And still I feel the snow in my soul,
silvery waterfalls and jagged peaks where birds
of prey glide through intoxicating air
and winds lash the snow and water.

Yes, I feel I am like the mountains.
My sadness has the same tone
as the gentians that bloom there.
In my family, plant collectors must have
buried themselves on boiling afternoons
with their insect-green boxes in the icy forest shade —
seeking precious samples they would not have traded
for marvellous Baghdad's ancient magic treasure
and sedating fountain breeze.
My love is tender as a rainbow
after April showers when the sunshine sings!
Why is my life like this? Was I not meant
to live on the summits amid clouds of snow
scattered by flocks of sheep
with a tall staff — expanding
into the peace of the breaking day.

23

Avec ton parapluie bleu et tes brebis

Avec ton parapluie bleu et tes brebis sales,
avec tes vêtements qui sentent le fromage,
tu t'en vas vers le ciel du coteau, appuyé
sur ton bâton de houx, de chêne ou de néflier.
Tu suis le chien au poil dur et l'âne portant
les bidons ternes sur son dos saillant.
Tu passeras devant les forgerons des villages,
puis tu regagneras la balsamique montagne
où ton troupeau paîtra comme des buissons blancs.
Là, des vapeurs cachent les pics en se traînant.
Là, volent des vautours au col pelé et s'allument
des fumées rouges dans des brumes nocturnes.
Là, tu regarderas avec tranquillité,
l'esprit de Dieu planer sur cette immensité.

Your Blue Umbrella

With your blue umbrella and dirty sheep
and clothes smelling of cheese, you head
up the hill and into the sky. Leaning
on your cane —holly, oak or medlar—
behind the shorthaired dog and donkey
carrying tarnished milk cans on his bony back—
you will pass the village blacksmiths
and enter the piney mountain where your flock—
like frosty bushes—will graze.

There, the peaks are shrouded in mist.
There, the scruffy vultures soar
and red smoke glows through the foggy night.
There, in peace you will watch God's spirit
gliding over the immensity.

Amie, souviens-toi

Amie, souviens-toi de ce jour où les prairies étaient de pierre,
où les vallées étaient mouillées par la lumière,
où les montagnes avaient les teintes de ces liqueurs
balsamiques fabriquées par des religieux.
C'était au soir et je sentais que s'élargissait mon cœur
vers la neige des hauts pics dorés, verts, et des pleurs
montaient à mes yeux en songeant au pays de mon enfance,
là-bas, vers l'air pur et froid, vers les neiges denses,
vers les montagnards, vers les bergers, vers les brebis,
vers les chèvres et les chiens gardiens et les flûtes
de buis que les mains calleuses rendent luisantes,
vers les cloches rauques des troupeaux piétinants,
vers les eaux éclusées, vers les tristes jardins,
vers les presbytères doux, vers les gamins
qui suivaient en chantant les conscrits qui chantaient,
vers les eaux d'été, vers les poissons blancs aux ailes rouges,
vers la fontaine de la place du village
où j'étais un petit garçon triste et sage.

Love, Do You Remember

Love, do you remember the day
the meadows turned stoney, the valleys
were slick with light and the mountains tinted
like balsamic liqueurs made by the monks.
It was evening — I felt my heart grow huge
and surge to the snow on peaks gold and green.
And tears came to my eyes as I pictured the country
of my childhood with its pure cold air, dense snows
and mountain people, shepherds, sheep,
goats and watch-dogs, wooden flutes
shined by callussed hands, the raucous bells
of grazing flocks — reservoirs, melancholy gardens
and sweet presbyteries, children singing
behind singing soldiers and summer streams,
white fish with red fins, and the fountain
in the square of the village where
I was a sad and good little boy.

Quand j'étais enfant

Quand j'étais enfant, l'école où j'allais
était le jardin du vieux presbytère
où les lys avaient l'odeur d'un mystère.
Elle était aussi le milieu des blés.
Elle était aussi, mon école douce,
près des vieux rosiers entourés de mousse.

Elle était aussi dans les carillons
qui rendent les champs plus mélancoliques.
C'est pourquoi mes vers sont des bucoliques
où se mêle un peu le cri des grillons.
Elle était aussi, douce Sainte-Vierge,
dans les fleurs de neige au long de la berge.

Elle était aussi dans les jours bénis
où les filles vont, fraîches et fleuries,
dépenser deux sous dans les loteries.
Elle était aussi dans les petits nids
qui flottent dans l'air, pareils à des bulles,
dans le ciel plus bleu qui les campanules.

Puis quand j'eus quitté mon tablier blanc
mon école fut auprès de mon père.
Mon école fut son regard austère.
Mais j'étais toujours l'enfant nonchalant,
l'enfant dont l'école était triste et douce
près des vieux rosiers entourés de mousse.

Puis mon cœur s'ouvrit à l'amour, soudain.
Un amour tout blanc, tout plein de mystère
comme les grands lys du vieux presbytère…
J'avais un génie ainsi qu'Aladin
et ma mie était pour moi la veilleuse
qui remplaçait la lampe merveilleuse.

Puis l'on m'a donné des cheveux, des fleurs.
Le temps a fané les fleurs bien-aimées.
Comme l'écureuil, le feu des ramées,
je m'en suis allé des branches en pleurs,
je m'en suis allé comme lui du chêne
rompant le cheveu qui faisait ma chaîne.

Je m'en suis allé, pauvre oiseau blessé.
J'ai quitté ma mie, et j'ai la blessure
qu'a faite à mon cœur sa douce figure.
Mon amour joli, que t'ai-je laissé?
De loin je t'envoie une larme douce
comme la rosée au fond d'une mousse.

Mon âme s'en va dans les carillons
qui rendent les champs plus mélancoliques.
C'est pourquoi mes vers sont des bucoliques
où se mêle un peu le cri des grillons.
Et je me souviens, douce Sainte-Vierge,
des lys blancs, pareils à vous, sur la berge…

When I Was a Child

When I was a child, the school
I attended was the old rectory garden
where lilies smelled of mystery.
Amidst the wheat it was —
my gentle school — and old roses
surrounded by moss.

And in the carillons that make
the meadows more melancholy.
That is why my verses are bucolic
and in them crickets chirp.
And it was in the snow-drops,
sweet holy Virgin, all along the banks.

And in the festive days when girls
fresh and fragrant, go to buy
a raffle for two pennies.
And in the little nests that float like bubbles
in the air — in skies bluer
than campanula.

When I no longer wore a white smock,
it was at my father's side —
his stern gaze my school.
But I remained a carefree child
with my sad gentle school

by the roses in the moss.

Then suddenly my heart opened to love!
Pure white and full of mystery
like the large lilies at the rectory.
I had a genie, like Aladdin.
My darling was my night-light—
the marvellous Lamp.

Locks of hair she gave me, and flowers—
precious blooms faded in time.
Like the squirrel, blazing
through the oak, I ran
from the branches weeping—
snapping the hair that bound me.

Poor injured bird, I fled
bearing the wound her sweet face
made in my heart.
My pretty love, why did I leave you?
From afar I send you a tear—
soft as the dew deep in the moss.

My soul peals with the carillons
that make the meadows melancholy.
That is why my verses are bucolic
and crickets chirp. And I remember,
sweet holy Virgin, lilies white
on the bank like you.

La maison serait pleine de roses

La maison serait pleine de roses et de guêpes.
On y entendrait, l'après-midi, sonner les vêpres;
et les raisins couleur de pierre transparente
sembleraient dormir au soleil sous l'ombre lente.
Comme je t'y aimerais! Je te donne tout mon cœur
qui a vingt-quatre ans, et mon esprit moqueur,
mon orgueil et ma poésie de roses blanches;
et pourtant je ne te connais pas, tu n'existes pas.
Je sais seulement que, si tu étais vivante,
et si tu étais comme moi au fond de la prairie,
nous nous baiserions en riant sous les abeilles blondes,
près du ruisseau frais, sous les feuilles profondes.
On n'entendrait que la chaleur du soleil.
Tu aurais l'ombre des noisetiers sur ton oreille,
puis nous mêlerions nos bouches, cessant de rire,
pour dire notre amour que l'on ne peut pas dire;
et je trouverais, sur le rouge de tes lèvres,
le goût des raisins blonds, des roses rouges et des guêpes.

Roses and Wasps

The house would be full of roses and wasps.
We would hear the bell ringing afternoon vespers.
Grapes like translucent stones would slumber
in the sun beneath the creeping shade.
And I would love you! Giving you all
my heart of twenty-four, my spirit of mockery,
my pride and poetry of white roses—
even though I do not know you, and you do not exist.
I only know that if you were alive and with me
down by the meadow—we would be kissing
and laughing under the golden bees, in the thick
leaves
along the cool stream. And hear nothing but
the heat of the sun. Your ear would be shaded
by the hazels, and our mouths would mingle—
ceasing their laughter—to say what can never
be said of our love. And I would discover
upon your red lips the taste of golden grapes,
red roses, and wasps.

Au moulin du bois froid

Au moulin du bois froid où coule de l'eau claire,
près des rochers, il y a de la fougère.

Tout près du bois bleu, une jeune fille blonde
lavait le linge et l'eau coulait à l'ombre.

Et elle avait retroussé sa robe assez haut :
on voyait ses jambes blanches dans l'eau.

Et les chemins étaient frais, étroits, mauvais, noirs,
comme si ç'avait été le soir.

Les chênes ronds et durs empêchaient la chaleur,
et, sur la mousse, il y avait des fleurs.

Nous marchions sur les petits cailloux des sentiers,
près des ronces rouges, des églantiers.

Parce qu'on dépiquait du froment, la batteuse
ronflait au soleil sur la paille creuse.

Mais je repasserai dans le bois où dans l'eau
une fille fraîche a la robe haut.

J'irai sur la noire et violette bruyère
couper avec effort de la fougère.

Est-ce que la nuit, quand il y a des étoiles,
    elle lave encore au ruisseau des toiles?

Pourquoi cela? —Bah! sur la bruyère violette,
    sur la fille chantera l'alouette.

Et je repasserai dans le bois où dans l'eau
    cette fille blanche a la robe haut.

Mill in the Cold Woods

At the mill in the cold woods where clear water
    flows, near the rocks there are ferns.

By those blue woods a fair-haired girl
    washed linens — water trickled in the shade.

She had pulled up her dress — her white legs
    could be seen in the water.

The paths were cool, narrow, rough and dark
    as if evening had fallen.

Round hard oaks kept out the heat;
    flowers bloomed on the moss.

We walked on a path of small stones
    by red bramble and sweet briar.

Wheat was being threshed — the thresher droned
    over empty straw in the sun.

But I will walk again through those woods
    where a young girl lifts her dress in water.

Over the black and violet moor I will go,
    chopping down ferns.

At night, below the stars, will she
    be washing her linens in the stream?

How can that be? Over the violet moor,
    above the girl, the lark will sing!

And I shall pass through those woods where
    a pale girl lifts her dress in the water.

Les dimanches

Les dimanches, les bois sont aux vêpres.
Dansera-t-on sous les hêtres?
Je ne sais... Qu'est-ce que je sais?
Une feuille tombe de la croisée...
C'est tout ce que je sais...

L'église. On chante. Une poule.
La paysanne a chanté, c'est la fête.
Le vent dans l'azur se roule.
Dansera-t-on sous les hêtres?
Je ne sais pas. Je ne sais.

Mon cœur est triste et doux.
Dansera–t-on sous les hêtres?
Mais tu sais bien que, les dimanches,
les bois sont aux vêpres.

Penser cela, est-ce être poète?
Je ne sais pas. Qu'est-ce que je sais?
Est-ce que je vis? Est-ce que je rêve?

Oh! ce soleil et ce bon, doux, triste chien...
Et la petite paysanne
à qui j'ai dit : vous chantez bien...

Dansera-t-elle sous les hêtres?
Je voudrais être, voudrais être

celui qui lentement laisse tomber,
comme un arbre ses baies,
sa tristesse pareille, sa tristesse
pareille aux bois qui sont aux vêpres.

On Sunday

On Sunday evening in the woods, it's vesper time.
Shall we dance under the beeches?
I don't know — what do I know?
A leaf falls from the vault —
that is all I know.

The church, a song, a hen —
the country girl singing — it's a festival!
Winds twirl in the azure.
Shall we dance under the beeches?
I don't know, I don't know.

Sad and gentle is my heart.
Will we dance under the beeches?
On Sunday evenings the woods
sing vespers.

Does thinking so make me
a poet? I do not know.
What do I know?
Am I alive or am I dreaming?

Oh the sun! The good sweet solemn
dog. And the country girl
I told, "You sing
beautifully."

Will she dance under the beeches?
If only I could shed my sorrows, sorrows
like a tree shedding berries,
like the woods singing vespers.

J'aime dans le temps

J'aime dans le temps Clara d'Ellébeuse,
l'écolière des anciens pensionnats,
qui allait, les soirs chauds, sous les tilleuls
lire les magazines d'autrefois.

Je n'aime qu'elle, et je sens sur mon cœur
la lumière bleue de sa gorge blanche.
Où est-elle? Où était donc ce bonheur?
Dans sa chambre claire il entrait des branches.

Elle n'est peut-être pas encore morte
—ou peut-être que nous l'étions tous deux.
La grande cour avait des feuilles mortes
dans le vent froid des fins d'Été très vieux.

Te souviens-tu de ces plumes de paon,
dans un grand vase, auprès de coquillages?...
on apprenait qu'on avait fait naufrage,
on appelait Terre-Neuve : le Banc.

Viens, viens, ma chère Clara d'Ellébeuse :
aimons-nous encore si tu existes.
Le vieux jardin a de vieilles tulipes.
Viens toute nue, ô Clara d'Ellébeuse.

Clara d'Ellébeuse

From the past, I love Clara d'Ellébeuse,
boarding school girl who strolled
under the lindens on warm evenings,
reading the magazines of old.

I love only her and feel on my heart
the blue light of her pale throat.
Where is she now? And where, that rapture?
The branches entered her bright room.

Maybe she is not dead, or maybe
we both were then. In the great courtyard
were dead leaves in the cold wind
at summer's end, so long ago.

Do you remember the peacock feathers
in the tall vase by the seashells?
A ship was wrecked, we heard,
on the sandbar of Newfoundland.

Come, come, dear Clara d'Ellébeuse.
Let us love again — if you exist.
The olden garden has olden tulips.
Come naked, oh Clara d'Ellébeuse.

Elle va à la pension

Elle va à la pension du Sacré-Cœur.
C'est une belle fille qui est blanche.
Elle vient en petite voiture sous les branches
des bois, pendant les vacances, au temps des fleurs.

Elle descend le coteau doucement. Sa charrette
est petite et vieille. Elle n'est pas très riche
et elle me rappelle les anciennes familles
d'il y a soixante ans, gaies, bonnes et honnêtes.

Elle me rappelle les écolières d'alors
qui avaient des noms rococos, des noms de livres
de distribution des prix, verts, rouges, olives,
avec un ornement ovale, un titre en or :

Clara d'Ellébeuse, Éléonore Derval,
Victoire d'Etremont, Laure de la Vallée,
Lia Fauchereuse, Blanche de Percival,
Rose de Liméreuil et Sylvie Laboulaye.

Et je pense à ces écolières en vacances
dans des propriétés qui produisaient encor,
mangeant des pommes vertes, des noisettes rances
devant le paon du parc frais, noir, aux grilles d'or.

C'était de ces maisons où il y avait table ouverte.
On y mangeait beaucoup de plats et on riait.
Par la fenêtre on voyait la pelouse verte
et la vitre, quand le soleil baissait, brillait.

Et puis un beau jeune homme épousait l'écolière
—une très belle fille qui était rose et blanche —
et qui riait quand au lit il baisait sa hanche.
Et ils avaient beaucoup d'enfants, sachants les faire.

Schoolgirls

She attends the school of the Sacred Heart—
that beautiful girl so white.
She comes in a small carriage under the branches,
during vacation when the flowers bloom.

She descends the hill gently. The carriage
is old and small. She is not very rich
and reminds me of the old families
sixty years ago, cheerful, good and honest.

She reminds me of the schoolgirls then,
with their rococo names, names of books
given as prizes—green, red and olive,
with oval ornament, title in gold:

Clara d'Ellébeuse, Éléonore Derval,
Victoire d'Etremont, Laure de la Vallée,
Lia Fauchereuse, Blanche de Percival,
Rose de Liméreuil and Sylvie Laboulaye.

I think of those schoolgirls during vacation
on farms still productive, eating green apples
and rancid hazelnuts in front of a peacock
in the cool shady park with gilded iron gates.

It was one of those houses with open table,
many dishes served, and everyone laughing.
Through the window, one saw the green grass
and as the sun went down, panes sparkled.

Then, a handsome youth married that schoolgirl —
so beautiful, pink and white — who laughed
on the bed when he kissed her hip. And knowing
how
to do it, they had many children.

J'étais gai

J'étais gai and l'église était calme au soleil,
près des jardins où sous la vigne il y a des roses,
près de la route où les oies et les canards causent,
les belles oies qui sont blanches comme du sel.

Sainte-Suzanne est le nom du petit village:
c'est un nom doux ainsi qu'un vieux nom de grand'mère.
L'auberge est pleine de fumée et de gros verres.
Les vieilles femmes n'y ont pas de babillage.

Il y a au soleil des chemins très obscurs,
pleins de feuillages frais et qui n'ont pas de fin.
On s'y donnerait des baisers longs, doux et durs,
par les après-midi des dimanches beaux et simples.

Je pense à tout cela. Alors une tristesse
me vient d'avoir laissé la femme que j'aimais.
J'avais vu autrement, alors, le mois de mai,
car mon coeur est fait pour aimer, aimer sans cesse.

Je sens que je suis fait pour un amour très pur
comme le soleil blanc qui glisse au bas du mur.
Et j'ai dans mon coeur des amours froids comme ceux
quand je passais ma main à travers ses cheveux.

Le soleil pur, le nom doux du petit village,
les belles oies qui sont blanches comme le sel,
se mêlent à mon amour d'autrefois, pareil
aux chemins obscurs et longs de Sainte-Suzanne.

48

Sainte Suzanne

I was happy, the church was silent in the sun
by a garden with roses under the vines
and a road where ducks and geese chatter,
beautiful geese as white as salt.

Sainte Suzanne is the name of that little village —
sweet as an old-fashioned grandmother's name.
The inn is full of smoke and heavy glasses.
Old women don't gossip there.

In the sunshine are dark paths
with fresh green leaves that lead on and on,
where one submits to long, soft and hard kisses
on beautiful simple Sunday afternoons.

I think of all that and a feeling of sorrow
comes over me, for I left the one I loved.
I saw May-time differently then, for my heart
is made to love and love incessantly.

I feel I am made for a love very pure —
like white sunlight sliding down a wall.
In my heart are cool loves —
like my fingers running through her hair.

The pure sunshine, the sweet name of that
little village, and the beautiful geese white as salt —
all mingle with my long-ago love
and the long dark paths of Sainte Suzanne.

C'était à la fin

C'était à la fin d'une journée bleue, tiède et claire.
Un piano chantait dans ces quartiers blancs et neufs
où les lauriers, les grilles, les sycomores trembleurs
font penser à des amours de pensionnaires.

Les vignes-vierges, comme des cordes de piments rouges,
rampaient dans le vent triste comme une flûte,
qui soufflait doucement dans le crépuscule,
à cette heure où, comme les cœurs, les feuilles bougent.

Mon âme, que ce soit le matin ou le soir,
aime les grands murs blancs qui ont des lèvres de roses.
Elle aime les portes fermées qui gardent des choses
qui s'enfoncent dans l'ombre où est la véranda.

Amaryllia se promentait à mon côté.
Soucieuse, elle saisit ma canne d'ébène,
comme en devaient avoir, au déclin des Étés,
les vieux rêveurs comme Bernardin de Saint-Pierre.

Elle me regarda et dit : « Comme je t'aime…
« Je ne me lasse pas de répéter ces mots…
« Dis-moi encore que tu m'aimes. « Je dis : « Je t'aime…»
Et mon cœur tremblait comme de noirs rameaux.

Il me sembla alors que mon amour pour elle
s'échappait en tremblant dans le jour rose et mûr,
et que j'allais fleurir, derrière les doux murs,
les sabres des glaïeuls dans les tristes parterres.

Vers elle je penchai ma lèvre, mais sans prendre
le baiser qu'elle s'attendait à recueillir.
Ce fut plus tendre encore qu'une guêpe chantante
qui voudrait sans vouloir se poser sur un lys.

C'était l'heure où l'on voit les premières lumières
éclairer la buée des vitres, dans les chambres
où, penchés sur un atlas clair, les écoliers
peignent l'Océanie avec des couleurs tendres.

Amaryllia me dit : « Ah! les petites riches…
« En voici deux qui rentrent avec l'institutrice…»
Alors mon cœur devint grave comme l'Évangile,
en entendant ces mots, et triste à en mourir.

Ô mon Dieu! Je crus voir, à plus de vingt ans de là,
la petite enfant que fut Amaryllia.
Ah! elle était sans doute un peu pauvre et malade…
Ô Amaryllia! Dis? Où est ton cartable?

Et, au moment où les enfants riches passèrent,
je me sentis trembler au bras de mon amie.
Mon cœur se contractait à la pensée d'un Christ
qui n'appelait à lui que les fils d'ouvriers.

The End

It was the end of a warm, clear blue day.
A piano was playing in one of the new white districts
where bay trees, iron grates, rustling sycamores
remind one of boarding school loves.

Virgin vines, resembling red peppers, were
creeping in the moody wind that whistled
softly, like a flute, in the dusk—the hour
when leaves and hearts are stirring.

Whether morning or evening, my soul
loves the large white walls lipped with roses,
the closed doors that guard things
under veranda shadows.

Amaryllia, walking beside me, carefully
placed her hand on my ebony cane—
like those Bernard de Saint Pierre and other
dreamers of old carried at summer's end.

Looking at me, she said: "I love you
and never tire of saying those words.
Tell me again you love me." "I love you,"
I said, my heart trembling like the dark trees.

Then it seemed that my love escaped rippling
into the ripe pink day, and in the sorry
soil behind those tender walls, spikes
of gladiolus would suddenly bloom.

Moving my lips toward her, I did not
pluck the kiss she was expecting —
and this was sweeter than a buzzing wasp
wanting, not wanting to settle on a lily.

It was the hour when the first lights
shine through steamy windows
of rooms where schoolboys bending over
a bright atlas, paint Oceania in soft colors.

"Ah, the little rich girls!" she said. "Here come
two, on their way home with their teacher."
Hearing her words, my heart turned grave
as the Gospel and deathly sad.

I thought I saw, over twenty years past,
the little child who was Amaryllia —
undoubtedly poor and sickly. Oh Amaryllia,
speak! Where is your school-bag?

As the rich children walked by,
I felt myself shaking on my beloved's arm.
My heart contracted at the thought of a Christ
who welcomed only the sons of workers.

Pourquoi les bœufs

Pourquoi les bœufs traînent-ils les vieux chars pesants?
Cela fait pitié de voir leur gros front bombé,
leurs yeux qui ont l'air de souffrance de tomber.
Ils font gagner le pain aux pauvres paysans.

S'ils ne peuvent plus marcher, les vétérinaires
les brûlent avec des drogues et des fers rouges.
Et puis dans les champs pleins de coquelicots rouges
les bœufs vont encore herser, racler la terre.

Il y en a qui se casse un pied quelquefois;
alors on tue celui-là pour la boucherie,
pauvre bœuf qui écoutait le grillon qui crie

et qui était obéissant aux rudes voix
des paysans qui hersaient sous le soleil fou,
pauvre bœuf qui allait il ne savait où.

Why Must Oxen

Why must oxen pull the heavy old carts?
Their large bulging brows and eyes of drop-dead
suffering, are painful to watch—as they
earn the poor peasants' daily bread.

When they can no longer walk—veterinarians
torture them with drugs and molten iron.
Then, through fields of red poppies,
they go on harrowing, raking the earth.

Sometimes one breaks a foot and
is slaughtered—for the butcher—
poor ox, who listened to the cricket
chirping and obeyed

the rude voices of the peasants
harrowing under the mad sun.
Poor ox, who never knew
where he was going.

C'était affreux

C'était affreux ce pauvre petit veau qu'on traînait
tout à l'heure à l'abattoir et qui résistait,

et qui essayait de lécher la pluie
sur les murs gris de la petite ville triste.

Ô mon Dieu! Il avait l'air si doux
et si bon, lui qui était l'ami des chemins en houx.

Ô mon Dieu! Vous qui êtes si bon,
dites qu'il y aura pour nous un pardon

—et qu'un jour, dans le Ciel en or, il n'y aura
plus de jolis petits veaux qu'on tuera,

et, qu'au contraire, devenus meilleurs,
sur leurs petites cornes nous mettrons des fleurs.

Ô mon Dieu! Faites que le petit veau
ne souffre pas trop en sentant entrer le couteau…

Poor Little Calf

It was awful—that poor little calf dragged
struggling to the slaughterhouse

who tried to lick rain from
the gray walls of this sad little town.

My God, he had an air so gentle and good,
he who loved the holly paths.

God, You who are good, tell us
that we will be pardoned

and one day in golden heaven no longer
kill pretty little calves

but rather, having become better,
will lay flowers on their small horns.

Oh my God! May the calf not suffer
too much as the knife enters…..

Cette personne

Cette personne a dit des méchancetés :
Alors j'ai été révolté.

Et j'ai été me promener près des champs
où les petits brins d'herbes ne sont pas méchants,
avec ma chienne et mon chien couchants.

Là, j'ai vu des choses qui jamais
n'ont dit aucune méchanceté,
et de petits oiseaux innocents et gais.

Je me disais, en voyant au-dessus des haies
s'agiter les tiges tendres des ronciers :
ces feuilles sont bonnes. Pourquoi y a-t-il des gens mauvais ?

Mais je sentais une grande joie
dans ce calme que tant ne connaissent pas,
et une grande douceur se faisait en moi.

Je pensais : oiseaux, soyez mes amis.
Petites herbes, soyez mes amies.
Soyez mes amies, petites fourmis.

Et là-bas, sur un champ en pente,
auprès d'une prairie belle et luisante
je voyais, près de ses bœufs, un paysan

qui paraissait glisser dans l'ombre claire
du soir qui descendait comme une prière
sur mon cœur calmé et sur la terre.

58

Friends

Someone spoke meanly —
and I was revolted....

With my aging dogs I went walking
by the fields — where little blades of grass
are never mean.

And there I saw the things that never
speak unkindly, and innocent
gay little birds.

Watching the blackberry stems
moving gently over the hedge, I thought:
They are good — why are there bad people?

But in that calm which many never know,
I felt a great joy, and a vast
sweetness rose within me.

I thought: Birds, be my friends.
Little grasses, be my friends.
Be my friends, little ants.

And on a nearby slope
by a beautiful radiant meadow,
I saw a farmer and his oxen slipping

into the soft evening shadow
that fell like a prayer
on my calmed heart and on the earth.

Le vent triste

Le vent triste souffle dans le parc,
comme dans un livre que je lus enfant,
où une écolière perdue était hagarde.
        Le vent.

Il va casser, peut-être, le tulipier.
Il fait voir le dessous des feuilles blanc
du vernis du japon qu'il semble essuyer,
        le vent.

Le baromètre est descendu subitement.
Peut-être que ça va être un ouragan.
Il ne peut pas pleuvoir, mais on entend
        le vent.

Dans les livres de prix, monsieur et madame d'Arvan
reviendraient en pressant le pas chez eux,
vers un château tout bleu malgré le mauvais temps.
        Le vent.

Sortez de ma tête, ô manoirs moisissants
où devaient se passer d'étranges adultères,
par les temps tristes, en Angleterre.
        Le vent.

Sortez de ma tête, gentilles écolières
qui jouiez à cache-cache dans la clairière,
et reveniez vers le grenier sombre, à cause du grand
        vent.

60

Sortez de ma tête, vieux marquis des villes
qui, dans les maisons pluvieuses, lisiez Virgile
dans des fauteuils à oreillettes, par des temps
de vent.

Sors de ma tête, ma douce tristesse,
et va-t'en vers le coteau fané, va-t'en
où va, sur un air un peu Chateaubriand,
le vent.

Sad Wind

The sad wind blows through the park—
as in a book I read as a child about
a wild-eyed schoolgirl lost.
   The wind.

Maybe it will crack the magnolia,
exposing the backs of leaves,
polishing them to a white Japanese lacquer—
   the wind.

Suddenly the barometer plunges—
maybe there will be a hurricane.
It won't rain but still you can hear
   the wind.

Mr. and Mrs. d'Arvan rushed home
to their castle—in prize books—pure blue
in spite of poor weather.
   The wind.

Get out of my head, moldy manors
where strange adulteries no doubt took place
in England in depressing weather.
   The wind.

Out of my head, nice schoolgirls
playing hide-and-seek in the clearing—
returning to their gloomy attic in strong
    wind.

Out of my head, old city marquis
reading Virgil in rained-on houses
in wing-backed chairs through seasons
    of wind.

Out of my head, sweet sorrow—away!
to the fading hills on a melody
like Chateaubriand—be gone with
    the wind.

La Salle à manger

Il y a une armoire à peine luisante
qui a entendu les voix de mes grand'tantes,
qui a entendu la voix de mon grand-père,
qui a entendu la voix de mon père.
A ces souvenirs l'armoire est fidèle.
On a tort de croire qu'elle ne sait que se taire,
car je cause avec elle.

Il y a aussi un coucou en bois.
Je ne sais pourquoi il n'a plus de voix.
Je ne veux pas le lui demander.
Peut-être qu'elle est cassée,
la voix qui était dans son ressort,
tout bonnement comme celle des morts.

Il y a aussi un vieux buffet
qui sent la cire, la confiture,
la viande, le pain et les poires mûres.
C'est un serviteur fidèle qui sait
qu'il ne doit rien nous voler.

Il est venu chez moi bien des hommes et des femmes
qui n'ont pas cru à ces petites âmes.
Et je souris que l'on me pense seul vivant
quand un visiteur me dit en entrant:
—comment allez-vous, monsieur Jammes?

Dining Room

There is a softly glowing cupboard
that listened to the voices of my great-aunts,
listened to the voice of my grandfather,
listened to the voice of my father.
And to their memory is faithful.
It is wrong to think her always silent—
for we talk.

There is a wooden cuckoo-clock as well.
I do not know why he has no voice.
And do not want to ask.
Maybe it broke—the voice
in his spring—just like
the voices of the dead.

There is also an old buffet
that smells of beeswax,
jam, meat, bread and ripe pears.
A loyal servant who knows
he must not steal anything.

Many men and women have come to visit
who do not believe in these little souls.
I smile when, thinking I live alone,
a visitor enters saying, "How are you,
Mr. Jammes?"

Il va neiger

Il va neiger dans quelques jours. Je me souviens
de l'an dernier. Je me souviens de mes tristesses
au coin du feu. Si l'on m'avait demandé : qu'est-ce?
J'aurais dit : laissez-moi tranquille. Ce n'est rien.

J'ai bien réfléchi, l'année avant, dans ma chambre,
pendant que la neige lourde tombait dehors.
J'ai réfléchi pour rien. A présent comme alors
je fume une pipe en bois avec un bout d'ambre.

Ma vieille commode en chêne sent toujours bon.
Mais moi j'étais bête parce que ces choses
ne pouvaient pas changer et que c'est une pose
de vouloir chasser les choses que nous savons.

Pourquoi donc pensons-nous et parlons-nous? C'est drôle;
nos larmes et nos baisers, eux, ne parlent pas
et cependant nous les comprenons, et les pas
d'un ami sont plus doux que de douces paroles.

On a baptisé les étoiles sans penser
qu'elles n'avaient pas besoin de nom, et les nombres
qui prouvent que les belles comètes dans l'ombre
passeront, ne les forceront pas à passer.

Et maintenant même, où sont mes vieilles tristesses
de l'an dernier? A peine si je m'en souviens.
Je dirais : laissez-moi tranquille, ce n'est rien,
si dans ma chambre on venait me demander: qu'est-ce?

When It Snows

In a few days, it will snow. I remember
last year — my sorrows by the fire.
If you had asked me what's wrong, I would
have said: Leave me alone, it's nothing.

I pondered deeply, last year,
in my room while the heavy snows fell.
I pondered for nothing — for I still
smoke a wooden pipe with an amber stem.

My old oak dresser smells as good as ever.
Oh yes, I was foolish, for nothing could be
changed — and we only pretend
to want to banish what is familiar.

Why, then, do we think and speak? It's odd —
our tears and kisses do not speak and yet
we understand them. The footsteps of a friend
are sweeter than the sweetest words.

We christened the stars without realizing
they needed no names. The numbers that
forecast beautiful comets crossing the dark,
will never make them appear.

And now, where have my old sorrows gone?
I barely remember them. If you came in
and asked me, what's wrong, I would say:
Leave me in peace, it's nothing,

Dieu (de La Naissance du Poète)

J'aime les hommes bons. Je plains l'homme mauvais.
J'aime les bonnes choses, les animaux et les plantes.
J'aime les révoltés, j'aime les résignés,
J'aime la Nuit, le Jour, le Soir et l'Aube blanche.

J'aime et ne demandez pas d'expliquer des choses.
Pourquoi voulez-vous que je vous les explique?
— Car c'est moi qui vous ai donné une logique,
et l'illogisme aussi, et le blé, et les roses.

J'aime. Aimez. Sans doute que j'ai eu raison…
Ne me demandez pas pourquoi une vipère
se fait tuer pour ses petits, en bonne mère.
A genoux! Les cœurs débordent de la raison.

God Speaks

I love good people and feel sorry for the wicked.
I love the good things, animals and plants.
I love the rebellious, love the resigned;
night, day, dusk and white dawn.

I love—and do not ask me to explain.
Why do you want an explanation?
I gave you reason and unreason—
the wheat as well as the rose.

I love. You should too. Surely I am right.
Do not ask why a viper—like any good mother—
offers her life for her young. Fall to your knees!
The heart goes beyond reason.

La paix est dans le bois

La paix est dans le bois silencieux et sur
les feuilles en sabre qui coupent l'eau qui coule,
l'eau reflète, comme en un sommeil, l'azur
pur qui se pose à la pointe dorée des mousses.

Je me suis assis au pied d'un chêne noir
et j'ai laissé tomber ma pensée. Une grive
se posait haut. C'était tout. Et la vie,
dans ce silence, était magnifique, tendre et grave.

Pendant que ma chienne et mon chien fixaient une
mouche qui volait et qu'ils auraient voulu happer,
je faisais moins de cas de ma douleur et laissais
la résignation calmer tristement mon âme.

Peace in the Woods

There is peace in the silent woods and
on sword leaves that cut the flowing water —
mirroring as in a dream, pure azure
poised on golden tips of moss.

I was sitting at the foot of a black oak
and let my thoughts go. A thrush lighted
above. That was all. And life in the silence
was magnificent, tender and grave.

While my dogs trapped a buzzing fly
they wanted to gobble, I dropped my case
for sorrow, and let resignation
wistfully calm my soul.

II. Prayer to Love Sorrow

Prière pour être simple

Les papillons obéissent à tous les souffles,
comme des pétales de fleurs jetés vers vous,
aux processions, par les petits enfants doux.
Mon Dieu, c'est le matin, et déjà, la prière
monte vers vous avec des papillons fleuris,
le cri du coq et le choc des casseurs de pierres.
Sous les platanes dont les palmes vertes luisent,
dans ce mois de juillet où la terre se craquèle,
on entend, sans les voir, les cigales grinçantes
chanter assidûment votre Toute-Puissance.
Le merle inquiet, dans les noirs feuillages des eaux,
essaie de siffler un peu longtemps, mais n'ose.
Il ne sait ce qu'il y a qui l'ennuie. Il se pose
et s'envole tout à coup en filant d'un seul trait,
à ras de terre, et du côté où l'on n'est pas.

Mon Dieu, tout doucement, aujourd'hui, recommence
la vie, comme hier et comme tant de fois.
Comme ces papillons, comme ces travailleurs,
comme ces cigales mangeuses de soleil,
et ces merles cachés dans le froid noir des feuilles,
laissez-moi, ô mon Dieu, continuer la vie
d'une façon aussi simple qu'il est possible.

Prayer to Be Simple

The butterflies surrender to every breath of air—
like the flower petals little children toss
at you during processions.
God, it is morning and prayers are already rising
toward you with the floral butterflies, the crowing
of the cock and stonecutters' hammering.
Under the plane tree's bright green palms
in the month of July when the earth is crackling—
we hear, though we cannot see, cicadas crunching,
diligently chanting your Omnipotence.
The restless blackbird in the dark river foliage
starts to whistle but does not quite dare.
Something bothers him—he perches and
suddenly darts, skimming over the dirt
to where there is no one.

My God, so gently life begins again today
as it did yesterday and every day before.
Like the butterflies, the workers, the cicadas
consuming the sun, and blackbirds hidden
in the cold dark leaves, may I too continue
to live, oh my God, as simply
as possible.

Prière pour avoir la foi dans la forêt

Je n'espère plus rien, mon Dieu, je me résigne.
Je sens la nuit sur moi comme elle est sur les champs,
quand le soleil s'éteint, le soir, comme une lampe.
Je ne vois plus en moi. Je suis comme le soir
qui fait qu'on ne voit plus les faneuses d'azur
à travers la prairie des pensées de mon âme.
Je voudrais être pareil au joli matin
où, dans la rosée rose, se peignent les lapins.
Je n'espère plus rien, mon Dieu, que le malheur,
et cela me rend doux comme l'agriculteur
qui suit patiemment la herse qui tressaute,
derrière, et au milieu des bœufs à cornes hautes.
Je suis abruti, mais c'est avec une grande douceur
que, du haut du coteau, dans la grande chaleur,
je regarde les bois luisants et noirs s'étendre
comme de grands morceaux de feuilles de silence.
Mon Dieu, peut-être que je croirais à vous davantage
si vous m'enleviez du cœur ce que j'y ai,
et qui ressemble à du ciel roux avant l'orage.
Peut-être, mon Dieu, que si vous me conduisiez
dans une chapelle bâtie au haut d'un arbre,
j'y trouvererais la foi solide comme du marbre.
Les geais d'azur feraient du ciel qui chanterait
dans la chaleur glacée de la grande forêt,
et ils boiraient dans la fraîcheur du bénitier.

Une petite cloche annoncerait, le soir,
un office, et un autre à l'heure des mésanges.
Dans cette église, il n'y aurait pas de jeunes femmes,
mais seulement des vieux, des enfants et des anges.
On y serait au ciel, puisque c'est sur des branches.
On n'y saurait plus rien, n'y penserait à rien...
Mais seulement, la nuit, quelquefois, le vieux chien
découvrirait le bon voyageur égaré.
O mon Dieu donnez-moi la foi dans la forêt.

Prayer for Faith in the Forest

Hope is gone and I am resigned, my God.
Night comes over me and covers the fields,
extinguishing the sun like a lamp. I see nothing
within. I am like the dusk that obscures
the harvesters of Azure on the prairie
of thoughts within my soul.
If only I were a lovely morning where
rabbits groom in the rosy dew.
I no longer expect anything, oh my God,
except misfortune, and that is humbling—
like a farmer who patiently follows the harrow
jerking behind the great-horned oxen.
I am stupified, and yet from the hilltop
in this intense heat, watch with tenderness
as the radiant black woods spread
their large leafy patches of silence.
My God, perhaps I would believe in you more
if you lifted from my heart this thing
that is like a russet sky before the storm.
If you carried me to a chapel on the top
of a tree, maybe I could find faith there,
solid as marble. In the icy warmth
of the forest, blue jays would create
a heaven of song, and drink fresh water
from your holy fount. A small bell
would announce a service at dusk,

another at the hour of the chickadees.
In that church, would be no young women —
only elders, children and angels.
We would be in heaven there — on the branches.
Know nothing but that! Think of nothing else.
Only once in a while — at night —
the old dog would discover
some good traveler gone astray.
Oh my God, give me faith in this forest!

Prière pour aimer la douleur

Je n'ai que ma douleur et je ne veux plus qu'elle.
Elle m'a été, elle m'est encore fidèle.
Pourquoi lui en voudrais-je, puisqu'aux heures
où mon âme broyait le dessous de mon cœur,
elle se trouvait là assise à mon côté?
O douleur, j'ai fini, vois, par te respecter,
car je suis sûr que tu ne me quitteras jamais.
Ah! Je le reconnais : tu es belle à force d'être.
Tu es pareille à ceux qui jamais ne quittèrent
le triste coin de feu de mon cœur pauvre et noir.
O ma douleur, tu es mieux qu'une bien aimée :
car je sais que le jour où j'agoniserai,
tu sera là, couchée dans mes draps, ô douleur,
pour essayer de m'entrer encore dans le cœur.

Prayer to Love Sorrow

I have only my sorrow and I want nothing more!
She has been and always will be faithful.
What more could I want, since at the very hour
when my soul demolished my heart —
she was there, seated at my side. Oh Sorrow —
look how I have finally come to respect you.
Because I know that you will never leave.
True, it was your persistence made you beautiful.
You are one of those who never abandoned
the sad hearth of my poor black heart.
Oh my Sorrow, you are better than a beloved!
For I know, when I draw my last breath,
wrapped in my sheets, you will be there —
Sorrow, still trying to invade my heart.

Prière pour louer Dieu

La torpeur de midi. Une cigale éclate
dans le pin. Le figuier seul semble épais et frais
dans le brasillement de l'azur écarlate.
Je suis seul avec vous, mon Dieu, car tout se tait
sous les jardins profonds, tristes et villageois.
Les noirs poiriers luisants, à forme d'encensoir,
dorment au long des buis qui courent en guirlandes
auprès des graviers blancs comme de Saintes-Tables.
Quelques jumbles labiées donnent une odeur sainte
à celui qui médite assis près des ricins.
Mon Dieu, j'aurais, jadis, ici, rêvé d'amour,
mais l'amour ne bat plus dans mon sang inutile,
et c'est en vain qu'un banc de bois noir démoli
demeure là parmi les feuillages des lys.
Je n'y mènerai pas d'amie tendre et heureuse
pour reposer mon front sur son épaule creuse.
Il ne me reste plus, mon Dieu, que la douleur
et la persuasion que je ne suis rien
que l'écho inconscient de mon âme légère
comme une effeuillaison de grappe de bruyère.
J'ai lu et j'ai souri. J'ai écrit, j'ai souri.
J'ai pensé, j'ai souri, pleuré et j'ai aussi
souri, sachant le monde impossible au bonheur,
et j'ai pleuré parfois quand j'ai voulu sourire.

Mon Dieu, calmez mon cœur, calmez mon pauvre cœur,
et faites qu'en ce jour d'été où la torpeur

s'étend comme de l'eau sur les choses égales,
j'aie le courage encore, comme cette cigale
dont éclate le cri dans le sommeil du pin,
de vous louer, mon Dieu, modestement et bien.

Prayer to Praise God

Noon torpor. The cicada
chirps in the pine. Only the fig still looks
fresh and healthy in the bright red sky.
I am alone with you now, my God — all is silent
under the deep sad village gardens.
Glowing black pear trees shaped like censors
doze by the boxwoods, that garland
the white gravel like a tabernacle.
A jumble of mint releases a holy scent
to the meditator seated by the castor plants.
In the past, I would have dreamed of love here,
but today, no love pulses through my useless blood.
The worn dark wood bench waits in vain
among the lilies. No fond happy friend
will I bring — to bury my face in the curve of her
neck.
All I have left, God, is this suffering and the belief
that I am nothing but the unconscious echo
of my soul, light as falling heather.
I read and I smiled. I wrote and I smiled.
I thought and smiled, wept and even then smiled —
understanding this world is not made for happiness —
and sometimes I wept when I wanted to smile.

Oh God, calm my heart, calm my poor heart
and on this summer day as torpor spreads like water

over everything—give me the courage
once again—like the cicada crying from the sleepy
                                        pine—
to praise you, my God—with modesty and grace.

Prière pour avouer son ignorance

Redescends, redescends dans ta simplicité.
Je viens de voir les guêpes travailler dans le sable.
Fais comme elles, ô mon cœur malade et tendre : sois sage,
accomplis ton devoir comme Dieu l'a dicté.
J'étais plein d'un orgueil qui empoisonnait ma vie.
Je croyais que j'étais bien différent des autres :
mais je sais maintenant, mon Dieu, que je ne fis
que récrire les mots qu'ont inventés les hommes
depuis qu'Adam et Ève au fond du Paradis
surgirent sous les fruits énormes de lumière.
Mon Dieu, je suis pareil à la plus humble pierre.
Voyez : l'herbe est tranquille, et le pommier trop lourd
se penche vers le sol, tremblant et plein d'amour.
Enlevez de mon âme, puisque j'ai tant souffert,
l'orgueil de me penser un créeur de génie.
Je ne sais rien. Je ne suis rien. Je n'attends rien
que de voir, par moments, se balancer un nid
sur un peuplier rose, ou, sur le blanc chemin
passer un pauvre lourd aux pieds luisants de plaies.
Mon Dieu, enlevez-moi l'orgueil qui m'empoisonne.
Oh! Rendez-moi pareil aux moutons monotones
qui passent, humblement, des tristesses d'Automne
aux fêtes du Printemps qui verdissent les haies.
Faites qu'en écrivant mon orgueil disparaisse:
que je me dise, enfin, que mon âme est l'écho
des voix du monde entier et que mon tendre père

m'apprenait patiemment des règles de grammaire.
La gloire est vaine, ô Dieu, et le génie aussi.
Il n'appartient qu'à Vous qui le donnez aux hommes
et ceux-ci, sans savoir, répètent les mêmes mots
comme un essaim d'été parmi de noirs rameaux.
Faites qu'en me levant, ce matin, de ma table,
je sois pareil à ceux qui, par ce beau Dimanche,
vont répandre à vos pieds dans l'humble église blanche
l'aveu modeste et pur de leur simple ignorance.

Prayer to Confess Ignorance

Return, return to your simplicity.
I have been watching the wasps working in the sand.
Do as they do, my sick tender heart—be good,
complete your duty, as dictated by God.
I was full of pride that poisoned my life—
thinking I was different from others—but now
I know, I was only re-writing the words
invented ever since Adam and Eve emerged
from Paradise, under fruit bulging with light.
Oh God, I am like the least of the stones.
Look! The grass is peaceful, the heavy apple tree
bows to the earth, trembling with love.
Remove from my soul—after so much pain—
the pride of thinking myself a creative genius.
I know nothing. Am nothing. Expect nothing
but to see now and then, a bird's nest balanced
on a pink poplar, or walking down the white road,
a poor bum whose wounded feet shine.
Remove, oh my God, this poisonous pride.
Make me like the monotonous sheep
who humbly go from Autumn sorrow
to Spring festivals where the bushes turn green.
May pride vanish from my words—and may
I finally know my soul echoes the voices
of the whole world, and my gentle father

patiently taught me the rules of grammar.
Glory is vain, my God, and so is genius.
It is yours alone to bestow upon humans
who unknowingly repeat the same words —
like summer bees swarming the dark branches.
Today as I rise from my table, make me
like those who, on this beautiful Sunday, offer
at your feet, in a humble white church, the pure
modest confession of their simple ignorance.

Élégie seconde

Les fleurs vont de nouveau luire au soleil pour moi.
Il semble que mon âme sorte d'un pays noir.
Trouverai-je la consolation sous les arbres?

Ma pipe est allumée comme à l'adolescence,
ma pipe est allumée dans le bruit de la pluie,
et je songe à des journées d'anciens printemps.

Des souvenirs chéris plus doux que des mélisses
habitent dans mon cœur joyeux et pourtant triste,
pareil à un jardin rempli de jeunes filles.

Car j'aime comparer à de très jeunes filles
mes pensées qui ont la courbe de leurs jambes craintives
et l'effarouchement moqueur d'éclats de rire.

Seules les jeunes filles ne m'ennuyèrent jamais :
Vous savez qu'elles vont, d'on ne sait quoi, causer
le long des tremblements de pluie des églantiers.

Et moi, je ne sais pas ce que mes pensées pensent.
J'aurais dû naître un jour calme des grandes vacances,
lorsque les framboisiers ont des cousines blanches.

Je ne sais pas pourquoi j'ai traversé la vie,
ni pourquoi, aujourd'hui, après ces grands ennuis,
je resonge à des soirs d'amour cachés de pluie.

Mon enfance est là-bas dans un petit parterre,
ma jeunesse un amour d'automne gris et vert,
et le reste sera l'yeuse du cimetière.

Peut-être que si Dieu ne m'a point fait mourir,
c'est qu'il s'est souvenu de toi, toute petite,
qui soignes, en m'attendant, tes jolis canaris.

Second Elegy (I)

The flowers will shine again in the sun.
I seem to be leaving some dark country.
Will there be solace under the trees?

My pipe burns as in adolescence,
it burns in the sound of the rain,
and I dream of spring days long ago.

In my sad and yet happy heart
are precious memories sweeter than melissa —
like a garden full of young girls.

Yes, I compare my thoughts to young girls
with their curving shy legs and fierce
bursts of mocking laughter.

Only young girls never bore me —
for you know they will always have something
to say, along the briar showering rain.

As for me, I don't know what my thoughts think.
I should have been born on a calm summer day
when raspberries have white cousins.

I do not know why I have traversed this life
or why today, after all my troubles,

I recall evenings of love hidden in the rain.

My childhood is over there — in a little flowerbed;
my youth — an autumn love, gray and green;
the rest — the oak in the cemetery.

If God has not taken me yet, perhaps
it is because he remembers you, so little,
waiting for me, tending your pretty canaries.

Élégie cinquième

Les anémones d'Octobre aux pelouses dorées
dorment. Des champignons troué par les limaces,
sont gluants dans la boue où des sangliers passèrent.
Les sorbiers des oiseaux saignent aux roux des bois.
Par moments, c'est après la pluie, le bois remue
tout entier, et ça fait comme s'il repleuvait :
les feuilles ruissellent et font un crépitement dru.

C'est la douceur d'Octobre et la pipe allumée.
Un rouge-gorge chante au boueux soleil pâle.
Je viens d'entrer dans le gris très doux de ma chambre.
Aujourd'hui le souvenir de mes chagrins est moins amer.
Je me revois tout jeune, en Octobre, à quatre heures,
quand j'étais écolier et que mon dictionnaire
avait des dates qui étaient des baisers.

Fifth Elegy

October anemones sleep in the golden grass.
Mushrooms pitted by slugs are slimy
in the mud where the wild boars passed.
Mountain ash bleed into the russet woods.
Sometimes, after rain, the whole forest
sways as if it were raining again—
leaves rustle and crackle loudly.

Sweet October with a smoking pipe—
red robin sings to the murky pale sun.
I have entered the soft gray of my room.
The memory of my sorrow is less bitter today.
I picture myself—young, in October, at four o'clock
when I was a schoolboy and the dates
in my encyclopedia were like kisses.

Élégie treizième

Lorsque l'on jouera de l'orgue pour nous seuls
         dans l'église,
elle aura des gouttes d'azur sous les cils,
         des larmes de bienheureuse.

Mais où est qui est assez pure
         pour mon âme qui est une cloche
d'église paysanne enfouie sous des aristoloches?
         Fiancée, où es-tu?

Ah! Si l'âme de mes roses blanches de juin
         souffle à tes lèvres de rose-Bengale :
lave ton corps, ô trembleuse, mets tes sandales
         et viens.

Quitte le monde amer et viens dans le cellule
         de mes recueillements,
d'où l'on entend courir l'eau vive sous les menthes
         que le soleil blanc consume.

Pour toi, j'ai préparé la fraîcheur verte de mes rêves
         où dorment des brebis.
Pour toi, j'ai un colier de cailloux blancs des grèves
         lavés à l'eau des puits.

Si tu arrives lasse, je m'agenouillerai
        et délierai tes sandales.
Tu n'auras qu'à laisser tomber sur mon épaule
        ta tête, et je te porterai.

La maison blanche emplie d'une rumeur dorée
        célébrera ta venue.
Ta sieste rêvera de la fraicheur des cruches,
        sur mon lit où je t'étendrai.

Et, pleurant d'amour, j'irai dans le blanc solstice,
        suivi de mes chiens harassés,
sonner la cloche en fleurs des plus pauvres églises
        pour annoncer la Fiancée.

Thirteenth Elegy

When the church organ plays
  just for us — under her eyelashes
will be drops of azure, tears
  of blessed joy.

But where is she who is pure enough
  for my soul that is a bell
in a pipevine-covered country church.
  Betrothed, where are you?

If the spirit of my white June roses
  reaches your Bengali-rose lips,
bathe your body, trembling,
  put on your sandals and come!

Leave the bitter world and come
  to my cell of meditation, where
you can hear the living waters, flowing
  under mint leaves, burning in the brilliant sun.

For you, I have prepared fresh green dreams
  where lambs slumber.
For you, a necklace of white river stones
  washed in well-water.

When you arrive, if you are tired,
   I will kneel and loosen your sandals.
Simply lean your head on my shoulder
   and I will carry you.

The white house will celebrate your coming
   in a golden clamor.
On the bed where I place you,
   fresh pitchers will fill your dreams.

And weeping with love in the white solstice,
   with my harried dogs I will go — to ring the bell
   in the flowers of a poor church —
   to announce our engagement.

Élégie quatorzième

—Mon amour, disais-tu. —Mon amour, répondais-je.
—Il neige, disais-tu. Je répondais : Il neige.

—Encore, disais-tu. —Encore, répondais-je.
—Comme ça, disais-tu. —Comme ça, te disais-je.

Plus tard, tu dis : Je t'aime. Et moi : Moi, plus encore...
—Le bel Été finit, me dis-tu. —C'est l'Automne,

répondis-je. Et nos mots n'étaient plus si pareils.
Un jour enfin tu dis : O ami, que je t'aime...

(C'était par un déclin pompeux du vaste Automne.)
Et je te répondis : Répète-moi... encore...

Fourteenth Elegy

My Love, you said. — My Love, I said.
It's snowing, you said. Snowing, I answered.

Again, you said. — Again, I answered.
Still, you said. — Still, I answered.

Later you said, I love you. And I said, more than
ever.
Lovely summer is ending, you spoke. — It's autumn,

I replied. And our words were no longer the same.
Finally you said, My dear, I love you so...

(as vast Autumn pompously descended).
And I said: Tell me again....

Élégie dix-septième

Il a plu. La terre fraîche est contente. Tout luit.
Une goute d'eau pèse et pend à chaque rose,
mais il va fair chaud, et, cet après-midi,
le soleil bourdonnant fendra la terrre rousse.
Le ciel brumeux se troue de bleus comme de l'eau
d'où des raies en travers tombent sur le coteau.
La taupe lisse, aux ongles forts, a rebouché
ses gîtes racineux qui pèlent la pelouse.
La limace argentée a traversé la route,
la fougère trempée est lourdement penchée,
and les ronces ont plu au cou des jeunes filles...

Car elles sont parties, les jeune filles, vers
ce qu'il y a de mouillé, de tremblant et de vert.
L'une avait son crochet, l'autre la bouche vive,
l'autre avait un vieux livre and l'autre des cerises,
l'autre avait oublié de faire sa prière.

—Lucie, regarde donc toutes ces taupinières?
—Oh! Que cette limace est laide. Ecrase-la.
—Oh! Horreur! Je te dis que non... Je ne veux pas.
—Ecoute, le coucou chante?

Elles sont allées
jusqu'au haut du chemin qui entre dans la lande.
Leurs robes s'écartaient et puis se raprochaient.
Les silences de leurs voix claires s'entendaient.

Une pie rayait longuement le ciel. Un geai
jacassait poursuivant un geai sur un noir chêne.
Ainsi qu'un éventail les robes s'écartèrent
encore, en ondulant, au soleil du sommet.
Elles ont disparu. Je m'en suis attristé.
Et, me sentant vieilli, j'ai pris dans le fossé,
je ne sais pas pourquoi, une tige de menthe.

Seventeenth Elegy

It rained. The fresh earth is content. Everything
sparkles. A drop of water hangs from each rose.
But it will be hot—afternoon's buzzing sun
will split apart the red and brown earth.
Through watery blue openings
in the mist, sunbeams strike the hill.
The sleek mole with his strong claws
has closed his rooty lodge, pushing up the grass.
The silver slug crossed the road,
ferns bend down soaked, and the bramble
has showered the necks of young girls....

For they went off—those girls—
into the wet and trembling green—one
with her crochet, another with her bright mouth,
another with an old book, another with cherries—
the other having forgotten her prayers.

—Lucy, look at the mole holes!
—Oh! That slug is so ugly—crush it!
—Horrors No, I will not!
—Listen, is that the cuckoo singing?

They have gone
to the crest of the hill where the moor begins.
Their dresses spread out and came together—

their clear voices blending in silence.
A magpie slowly veered in the sky. A jay
squawked after another jay in the black oak.
Again their dresses fanned, undulating in the light
on the summit. Then they disappeared.
And I was sad. Feeling older, I picked
from the ditch, who knows why,
a sprig of mint.

Élégie première

Mon cher Samain, c'est à toi que j'écris encore.
C'est la première fois que j'envoie à la mort
ces lignes que t'apportera, demain, au ciel,
quelque vieux serviteur d'un hameau éternel.
Souris-moi pour que je ne pleure pas. Dis-moi :
« Je ne suis pas si malade que tu le crois. »
Ouvre ma porte encore, ami. Passe mon seuil
et dis-moi en entrant : « Pourquoi es-tu en deuil? »
Viens encore. C'est Orthez où tu es. Bonheur est là.
Pose donc ton chapeau sur la chaise qui est là.
Tu as soif? Voici de l'eau de puits bleue et du vin.
Ma mère va descendre et te dire : « Samain…»
et ma chienne appuyer son museau sur ta main.

Je parle. Tu souris d'un sérieux sourire.
Le temps n'existe pas. Et tu me laisses dire.
Le soir vient. Nous marchons dans la lumière jaune
qui fait les fins du jour ressembler à l'Automne.
Et nous longeons le gave. Une colombe rauque
gémit tout doucement dans un peuplier glauque.
Je bavarde. Tu souris encore. Bonheur se tait.
Voici la route obscure au déclin de l'Été,
voici que nous rentrons sur les pauvres pavés,
voici l'ombre à genoux près des belles-de-nuit
qui ornent les seuils noirs où la fumée bleuit.

104

Ta mort ne change rien. L'ombre que tu aimais,
où tu vivais, où tu souffrais, où tu chantais,
c'est nous qui la quittons et c'est toi qui la gardes.
Ta lumière naquit de cette obscurité
qui nous pousse à genoux par ces beaux soirs d'Été
où, flairant Dieu qui passe et fait vivre les blés,
sous les liserons noirs aboient les chiens de garde.

Je ne regrette pas ta mort. D'autres mettront
le laurier qui convient aux rides de ton front.
Moi, j'aurais peur de te blesser, te connaissant.
Il ne faut pas cacher aux enfants de seize ans
qui suivront ton cercueil en pleurant sur ta lyre,
la gloire de ceux-là qui meurent le front libre.

Je ne regrette pas ta mort. Ta vie est là.
Comme la voix du vent qui berce les lilas
ne meurt point, mais revient après bien des années
dans les mêmes lilas qu'on avait cru fanés,
tes chant, mon cher Samain, reviendront pour bercer
les enfants que déjà mûrissent nos pensées.

Sur ta tombe, pareil à quelque pâtre antique
dont pleure le troupeau sur la pauvre colline,
je chercherais en vain ce que je peux porter.
Le sel serait mangé par l'agneau des ravines
et le vin serait bu par ceux qui t'ont pillé.

Je songe à toi. Le jour baisse comme ce jour
où je te vis dans mon vieux salon de campagne.
Je songe à toi. Je songe aux montagnes natales.
Je songe à ce Versailles où tu me promenas,

où nous disions des vers, tristes et pas à pas.
Je songe à ton ami et je songe à ta mère.
Je songe à ces moutons qui, au bord du lac bleu,
en attendant la mort bêlaient sur leurs clarines.
Je songe à toi. Je songe au vide pur des cieux.
Je songe à l'eau sans fin, à la clarté des feux.
Je songe à la rosée qui brille sur les vignes.
Je songe à toi. Je songe à moi. Je songe à Dieu.

First Elegy

My dear Samain, I am still writing to you.
For the first time I send death these lines
some old servant in a timeless hamlet
will deliver to you tomorrow in heaven.
Smile for me, so I will not cry.
Say, "I am not as sick as you think."
Open the door, dear friend. And step over
the threshold saying, "Why are you in mourning?"
Come back to Orthez. Where there is joy.
Place your hat on the chair. Are you thirsty?
There is blue water from the well and wine.
Mother will come down greeting you, "Samain!"
And my dog place her nose in your hand.

I talk, you smile your serious smile.
Time does not exist. You let me speak.
Evening approaches. We walk in the yellow light
that makes the end of the day feel autumnal.
We stroll by the stream. A rasping dove moans softly
in the blue gray poplar. I chatter on.
You smile again. The joy is silent.
The road is dim at the end of summer;
here we return on worn cobble stone;
here a shadow crouches by night-blooming lilies
near the dark thresholds with blue vapors.

Your death changes nothing.
The shadow you loved—where you lived
and suffered and sang—we will leave,
but you will keep guarding it.
Your light was born from that darkness
which brings us to our knees on beautiful summer
                                                    evenings
when watch-dogs—smelling God enlivening
the grains—bay under the black bindweed.

I do not regret your death. Let others
place the laurel, honoring your aged brow.
I, knowing you, would be afraid of hurting you.
We must not hide from the young who follow your
                                                    coffin
weeping over your lyre, the glorious faces
of those who die free.

I do not regret your death. Your life is there.
As the vocal wind, shaking the lilacs,
does not die but returns years later
to the same lilacs we thought dying,
your songs, dear Samain, will return and shake
the children whom our thoughts now nurture.

Like some ancient herder whose flock weeps
on the wretched slope, I search in vain
for something to bring to your grave.
Salt would be eaten by the sheep of the ravines
and wine drunk by those who robbed you.

I dream of you. The sun sets as it did that day
when you appeared in my old country parlor.
I dream of you. I dream of our native mountains.
I dream of Versailles where you took me step
by step reciting melancholy verses.
I dream of your friend and your mother.
Dream of lambs bleating, clanging at the edge
of the blue lake, awaiting death.
I dream of you. I dream of the pure emptiness
of the skies. Dream of unending water and firelight
and dew sparkling on the vines.
I dream of you. I dream of me. I dream of God.

Je ne veux pas d'autre joie

Je ne veux pas d'autre joie, quand l'été
reviendra, que celle de l'an passé.
Sous les muscats dormants, je m'assoirai.
Au fond des bois qui chantent de l'eau fraîche,
j'écouterai, je sentirai, verrai
tout ce qu'entend, sent et voit la forêt.

Je ne veux pas d'autre joie, quand l'automne
reviendra, que celle des feuilles jaunes
qui racleront les coteaux où il tonne,
que le bruit sourd du vin neuf dans les tonnes,
que les ciels lourds, que les vaches qui sonnent,
que les mendiants qui demandent l'aumône.

Je ne veux pas d'autre joie, quand l'hiver
reviendra, que celle des cieux de fer,
que la fumée des grues grinçant en l'air,
que les tisons chantant comme la mer,
et que la lampe au fond des carreaux verts
de la boutique où le pain est amer.

Je ne veux pas, quand revient le printemps,
d'autre joie que celle de l'aigre vent,
que les pêchers sans feuilles fleurissants,
que les sentiers boueux et verdissants,
que la violette et que l'oiseau chantant
comme un ruisseau d'orage se gorgeant.

No Other Joy

I want no other joy when the summer
returns, than that of the year gone by.
Under dozing muscats I shall sit.
Deep in the woods, where fresh waters sing,
I will hear and feel and see everything
the forest hears, feels and sees.

I want no other joy when the autumn
returns, than that of the yellow leaves
raking the hills when it thunders,
than the dull sound of new wine in barrels,
than heavy skies and cowbells ringing
and beggars asking for alms.

I want no other joy when the winter
returns, than that of the iron sky,
than the smoke of the grinding cranes,
than embers singing like the sea,
than the lamp behind green panes
in the shop where the bread is bitter.

I want no other joy when the spring
returns, than that of the biting winds,
than peach trees, leafless, blooming,
than muddy paths turning green,
than the violet, than the bird singing
like a stream that gorges in the storm.

J'ai déjeuné chez un ami...

J'ai déjeuné chez un ami. Des camélias
commencent à jaunir le mur de sa villa.
Voilà longtemps que nous nous connaissons. Déjà
le printemps trop hâtif fleurit le leycestria
sous lequel, en Eté, nous causons lui et moi.

Sous l'aigre vent de pluie les carcasses des arbres
agaçaient mes regards qui désiraient revoir
les feuilles de Juillet à la mollesse bleue.

Peut-être que, l'Eté, sous le leycestria,
nos cœurs regretteront cet après-midi noir
qui nous a fait longtemps rester au coin du feu.

At My Friend's

I had lunch at a friend's. Camellias
were starting to turn the villa walls creamy.
We have been friends a long time. In the early spring
blossoms are already appearing on the wisteria
under which we chat in summer.

In the bitter rainy wind, the skeletons
of the trees were painful to my eyes that yearned
for the leaves and blues of gentle July.

Maybe, come summer, under the wisteria,
our hearts will miss this gloomy afternoon
that kept us so long by the fire.

L'enfant lit l'almanach

L'enfant lit l'almanach près de son panier d'oeufs.
Et, en dehors des Saints et du temps qu'il fera,
elle peut contempler les beaux signes des cieux:
Chèvre, Taureau, Bélier, Poissons, et caetera.

Ainsi peut-elle croire, petite paysanne,
qu'au-dessus d'elle, dans les constellations,
il y a des marchés pareils avec des ânes,
des taureaux, des béliers, des chèvres, des poissons.

C'est le marché du Ciel sans doute qu'elle lit.
Et, quand la page tourne au signe des Balances,
elle se dit qu'au Ciel comme à l'épicerie
on pèse le café, le sel et les consciences.

Child Reading an Almanac

A child reads the almanac by her basket of eggs.
Along with saints and weather forecasts
are beautiful heavenly signs to contemplate:
Capella, Taurus, Aires, Pisces, etcetera.

And so she imagines, the little peasant girl,
above her, among the constellations,
similar markets—with donkeys,
bulls, rams, goats, and fish.

She studies Heaven's market
and when she turns the page to the Scales,
concludes that in Heaven—like the grocery—
they weigh coffee, salt and consciences.

Je ne m'y trompe pas...

Je ne m'y trompe pas. Hier, à la nuit tombante,
dans l'ombre des coteaux sonore et forestière,
j'ai entendu déjà ce chant particulier
du merle imitateur lorsque vient le printemps.

Ce chant semble gonflé de sèves roucoulantes
comme les gorgées d'eau de carafes de terre.
Ce matin les moineaux ont leurs voix printanières,
la même qu'ils avaient lorsque j'étais enfant.

Ainsi que la saison indécise, j'hésite...
Je ne sais trop si c'est le printemps ou l'hiver;
cela dépend de vous, mais il faut faire vite:
la giroflée marronne aime le vent de mer.

I Am Certain

I am sure of it. Yesterday as night was falling,
in the shade of sonorous wooded hills,
I heard that special song the mocking bird
sings when spring arrives.

Song swollen with gurgling sap —
like water gulped from earthen pitchers.
This morning, the sparrows have their spring
voices —
just as when I was young.

Like the indecisive season, I hesitate,
uncertain whether it is spring or winter.
That depends on you, but we must hurry —
the wild gilliflower loves the ocean breeze.

C'est un coq...

... *C'est un coq dont le cri taille à coups de ciseaux*
l'azur net qui s'aiguise au tranchant du coteau.
Mais je veux autre chose encore?

... *C'est la salle à manger sur un parc, à midi.*
Une femme en blanc, lourde et blonde, pèle un fruit.
—Je veux voir autre chose encore?

... *C'est une eau tendrement aimée par le village*
qui s'y mire et dénoue sur elle ses feuillages.
—Je veux voir autre chose encore?

... *Mais quoi donc? – Oh! Tais-toi, car je souffre! Je veux*
je veux voir, je veux voir au-delà de mes yeux
je ne sais quelle chose encore...

That is a Rooster

That is a rooster whose cry cuts, like scissors,
the clear blue—that sharpens on the hill's edge.
     But I want something else?

That is a dining room over a park at noon.
A woman in white, plump and blond, peels fruit.
     —I want to see something else?

That is a river loved by the village that gazes
in its mirror and showers it with leaves.
     —Want to see something else?

What then? —Oh hush, this hurts! I want
want to see, want to see further than eyes can see—
     I don't know what else....

O mon Ange gardien

O mon Ange gardien, toi que j'ai laissé là
pour ce beau corps blanc comme un tapis de lilas :
Je suis seul aujourd'hui. Tiens ma main dans ta main.

O mon Ange gardien, toi que j'ai laissé là
quand ma force éclatait dans l'Eté de ma joie :
Je suis triste aujourd'hui. Tiens ma main dans ta main.

O mon Ange gardien, toi que j'ai lassé là
quand je foulais d'un pied prodigue l'or des bois :
Je suis pauvre aujourd'hui. Tiens ma main dans ta main.

O mon Ange gardien, toi que j'ai laissé là
quand je rêvais devant la neige sur les toits.
Je ne sais plus rêver. Tiens ma main dans ta main.

Guardian Angel

Oh, my guardian Angel whom I left
for that lovely body white as a carpet of lilacs.
Today I am alone—take my hand in yours.

Oh, my guardian Angel whom I left
when my force exploded in that summer of joy.
Today I am sad—take my hand in yours.

Oh, my guardian Angel whom I left
when my prodigal foot discovered the gold of forests.
Today I am poor—take my hand in yours.

Oh, my guardian Angel whom I left
as I dreamed under rooftops covered in snow.
I no longer dream—take my hand in yours.

Dans ce site où la Sainte Vierge est apparue

Dans ce site où la Sainte Vierge est apparue,
la roche et le galet sont lustrés par l'eau crue
qui mire une lumière aveuglante, brisée
par ces cristaux d'air bleu appelés Pyrénées.
La flore est composée d'espèces balsamiques,
et la faune d'agneaux aperçus de si bas
qu'il semble que ce soit dans l'azur qu'ils cheminent.
Ainsi qu'un long soupir on entend un cantique
monter de la Douleur des douleurs qui sont là.

C'est près du vert torrent, dans le coin d'une grotte,
que la Vierge, vêtue de neige et de ciel bleu,
comme une eau descendue d'une céleste roche
jasa vers une enfant pauvre comme son Dieu.
Grottes de Bethléem et du Gethsémani,
fontaines d'abondance, on vous retrouve ici!

Agenouillé dans l'ardente grotte enfumée,
dans la terrible joie de son humilité,
pareil à ces manants qui ne savent pas lire,
laissant loin la raison savante qui délire,
le poète reçoit la vie telle qu'elle est.

Et il comprend, en regardant ces faces rustres
et ces mains de terreau semant des chapelets,
que c'est dans cette Foi pauvre, nue et robuste,
qu'entre, pour l'habiter comme une crèche, Dieu.

122

The Virgin Appeared

At the site where the Holy Virgin appeared,
rock and stones are glazed by the hard water
that reflects a blinding light, broken
by this crystal blue air we call *Pyrenees*.
The flora consists of balsamic species,
the fauna of sheep who appear,
from down below, to wander in the sky.
In a drawn-out sigh, a canticle rises
from the Sorrow of all the sorrows present here.

It was near this green waterfall, deep in a grotto,
that the Virgin, draped in snow and blue sky,
babbled like a stream from heavenly rock
to a child as poor as her God.
Grottos of Bethlehem and Gethsemane,
fountains of abundance, discovered here too!

Upon his knees in the hot smoky grotto,
in the terrible joy of his humility,
like these peasants who do not know how to read,
the poet leaves his clever, raving reason
and takes life as it really is.

And gazing at their rustic faces
and mouldy hands sowing prayer beads,
he understands that this poor, naked, robust Faith
is the manger where God enters and dwells.

Mon humble ami, mon chien fidèle

Mon humble ami, mon chien fidèle, tu es mort
de cette mort que tu fuyais comme une guêpe
lorsque tu te cachais sous la table. Ta tête
s'est dirigée vers moi à l'heure brève et morne.

O compagnon banal de l'homme : Etre béni!
toi que nourrit la faim que ton maître partage,
toi qui accompagnas dans leur pèlerinage
l'archange Raphaël et le jeune Tobie…

O serviteur : Que tu me sois d'un grand exemple,
ô toi qui m'as aimé ainsi qu'un saint son Dieu!
Le mystère de ton obscure intelligence
vit dans un paradis innocent et joyeux.

Ah! faites, mon Dieu, si Vous me donnez la grâce
de Vous voir face à Face aux jours d'Eternité,
faites qu'un pauvre chien contemple face à face
celui qui fut son dieu parmi l'humanité.

My Faithful Dog

Humble friend, faithful dog, you died
of that death you tried to escape, hiding
under the table as if it were a wasp.
Your head turned to me in that brief sad hour.

Daily companion of man, blessed being!
Nourished by a hunger shared with your master,
you accompanied the archangel Raphael
and young Tobias on their journey.

Oh my servant, may you who loved me as only
a saint loves his God, be for me a great example.
The mystery of your obscure intelligence
lives in a paradise of innocence and joy.

Oh my God, if some day in eternity
by your grace, I meet You face to Face —
let a poor dog contemplate, face to face,
the one who was his god among humanity.

Au crépuscule

Au crépuscule, à l'heure où le silence saint
de la chapelle, par un mariage divin,
s'unit aux boiseries qu'orne un chemin de croix,
enfumée du parfum des encens séculaires…
quand l'ombre rejoint l'eau dans le bénitier froid…
quand le vent pleure bas autour du presbytère
dans les tristes rameaux de peupliers carolins…
quand le dernier rayon dore de son mystère
l'althaea rose auprès duquel lit son bréviaire
un humble desservant qui va vers son déclin…

Alors, sortant de la chapelle où l'a mené
sa rêverie errante, le poète a refermé
la grille. On voit la lune en métal bosselé.
L'âme garde longtemps le parfum du rosaire
comme la boîte verte garde une odeur de feuilles.
Certe il est bon, quand la Terre vous abandonne,
de méditer, et qu'alors le Ciel vous accueille.
Il est bon, quand sur soi l'orage couve et tonne,
de descendre dans la profondeur des Mystères;
il est bon lorsque les hommes vous ont trahi,
quand on est exilé, quand on n'est pas compris,
de retrouver toujours la Famille divine.
Cette Famille est là, qui avec vous chemine
ou s'arrête avec vous, matin, midi et soir;
il est bon de parler à la Vierge et la voir,
tantôt enfant, avec son voile dans le Temple,

pure comme elle-même et remplissant sa lampe;
tantôt tranquillement belle, puissamment mère;
tantôt vieille, voûtée et saintement amère.
Il est bon d'évoquer son Enfant glorieux
et, banni par les hommes, d'habiter avec Dieu.

Twilight

At twilight, the hour when the sacred silence
of the chapel fills with the fragrance
of worldly incense and joins the woods
in divine marriage, marked with stations of the Cross;
when the shadow merges with the cold water
of the font; and the wind moans around the rectory
in the sorrowing poplars; and the pink hollyhock
is gilded in mystery by the last rays;
and a humble parish priest nearing his end
reads nearby from his breviary.

Then the poet leaves the chapel
where his wandering reverie brought him,
closing the iron gate. The moon shines
on wrought metal. The soul guards the fragrance
of the rosary for a long time — as a green box holds
onto the scent of leaves. When the Earth
abandons you, it is good to meditate
so that Heaven may receive you.
It is good, when storms gather and thunder,
to descend deep into the Mysteries;
good, when men betray you and you are exiled
and misunderstood, to rediscover the holy Family —
the family that walks and pauses beside you —
morning, noon and night. Good to talk
to the Virgin and see her — whether as a girl

veiled, in the temple, perfectly pure, filling her lamp;
or serenely beautiful, powerfully maternal;
or old, devout and bitter—like a saint.
It is good to invoke her glorious Child
and, banished by men, to live with God.

Rosaire

Annonciation.

Par l'arc-en-ciel sur l'averse des roses blanches,
par le jeune frisson qui court de branche en branche
et qui a fait fleurir la tige de Jessé;
par les Annonciations riant dans les rosées
et par les cils baissés des graves fiancées :
    Je vous salue, Marie.

Visitation.

Par l'exaltation de votre humilité
et par la joie du cœur des humbles visités;
par le Magnificat qu'entonnent mille nids,
par les lys de vos bras joints vers le Saint-Esprit
et par Elisabeth, treille où frémit un fruit :
    Je vous salue, Marie.

Nativité.

Par l'âne et par le bœuf, par l'ombre et par la paille,
par la pauvresse à qui l'on dit qu'elle s'en aille,
par les nativités qui n'eurent sur leurs tombes
que les bouquets du givre aux plumes de colombe;
par la vertu qui lutte et celle qui succombe :
    Je vous salue, Marie.

Purification.

Par votre modestie offrant des tourterelles,
par le vieux Siméon pleurant devant l'autel,
par la prophétesse Anne et par votre mère Anne,
par l'obscur charpentier qui, courbé sur sa canne,
suivait avec douceur les petits pas de l'âne :
                    Je vous salue, Marie

Invention de Notre Seigneur au Temple.

Par la mère apprenant que son fils est guéri,
par l'oiseau rappelant l'oiseau tombé du nid,
par l'herbe qui a soif et recueille l'ondée,
par le baiser perdu, par l'amour redonné,
et par le mendiant retrouvant sa monnaie :
                    Je vous salue, Marie.

Agonie.

Par le petit garçon qui meurt près de sa mère
tandis que des enfants s'amusent au parterre;
et par l'oiseau blessé qui ne sait pas comment
son aile tout à coup s'ensanglante et descend;
par la soif et la faim et le délire ardent:
                    Je vous salue, Marie.

Flagellation.

Par les gosses battus par l'ivrogne qui rentre,
par l'âne qui reçoit des coups de pied au ventre,
par l'humiliation de l'innocent,
par la vierge vendue qu'on a déshabillée,
par le fils dont la mère a été insultée :
   Je vous salue, Marie.

Couronnement d'épines.

Par le mendiant qui n'eut jamais d'autre couronne
que le vol des frelons, amis des vergers jaunes,
et d'autre sceptre qu'un bâton contre les chiens;
par le poète dont saigne le front qui est ceint
des ronces des désirs que jamais il n'atteint :
   Je vous salue, Marie.

Portement de Croix.

Par la vieille qui, trébuchant sous trop de poids,
s'écrie « Mon Dieu! » Par le malheureux dont les bras
ne purent s'appuyer sur une amour humaine
comme la Croix du Fils sur Simon de Cyrène;
par le cheval tombé sous le chariot qu'il traîne :
   Je vous salue, Marie.

Crucifiement.

Par les quatre horizons qui crucifient le Monde,
par tous ceux dont la chair se déchire ou succombe,
par ceux qui sont sans pieds, par ceux qui sont sans mains,
par le malade que l'on opère et qui geint
et par le juste mis au rang des assassins :
   Je vous salue, Marie.

Résurrection.

Par la nuit qui s'en va et nous fait voir encore
l'églantine qui rit sur le cœur de l'aurore;
par la cloche pascale à la voix en allée
et qui, le Samedi-Saint, à toute volée,
couvre d'alleluias la bouche des vallées :
   Je vous salue, Marie.

Ascension.

Par le gravissement escarpé de l'ermite
vers les sommets que les perdrix blanches habitent,
par les troupeaux escaladant l'aube du ciel
pour ne se nourrir plus que de neige de miel,
et par l'Ascension du glorieux soleil :
   Je vous salue, Marie.

Pentecôte.

Par les feux pastoraux qui descendent, la nuit,
sur le front des coteaux, ces apôtres qui prient;
par la flamme qui cuit le souper noir du pauvre;
par l'éclair dont l'Esprit allume comme un chaume,
mais pour l'Eternité, le néant de chaque homme :
Je vous salue, Marie.

Assomption.

Par la vieille qui atteint, portant un faix de bois,
le sommet de la route et l'ombre de la Croix,
et que son plus beau fils vient aider dans sa peine;
par la colombe dont le vol à la lumière
se fond si bien qu'il n'est bientôt qu'une prière :
Je vous salue, Marie.

Couronnement de la Sainte Vierge.

Par la Reine qui n'eut jamais d'autre Couronne
que les astres, trésor d'une ineffable Aumône,
et d'autre sceptre que le lys d'un vieux jardin;
par la vierge dont penche le front qui est ceint
des roses des désirs que son amour atteint :
Je vous salue, Marie.

Hail Mary

Annunciation

By the rainbow, over a shower of white roses;
by the new pulse stirring in the branches
that made Jesse's branch bloom;
by the Annunciations laughing in the dew
and the lowered eyelids of solemn fiancées:
    I salute you, Mary.

Visitation

By the exaltation of your humility,
the gladdened hearts of the humble visited,
and the Magnificat ringing from a thousand nests;
by your arms full of lilies, lifted to the Spirit,
and Elisabeth, trellis of trembling fruit:
    I salute you, Mary.

Nativity

By the donkey and the cow, the shade
and the straw, the poor woman told to go away,
the dead with only bunches of frosted dove feathers

to mark their graves; by the virtue that struggles
and the virtue that succumbs:
    I salute you, Mary.

Purification

By your modest offering of turtle doves
and old Simeon weeping at the altar;
by Anne the prophet and Anne your mother,
and the unknown carpenter bent over his cane,
softly following the steps of a donkey:
    I salute you, Mary.

Our Lord Entering the Temple

By the mother realizing her son is cured,
the bird calling from her nest to the fallen,
the parched grass drinking the rain;
by the kiss that was lost, the love that returned,
and the beggar finding his change:
    I salute you, Mary.

Agony

By the little boy dying at his mother's side
while children play in the garden;
by the wounded bird who does not know why

his bloody wing falls; by the thirst
and the hunger and the burning fever:
    I salute you, Mary.

Flagellation

By the kids beaten when the drunk comes home,
and the donkey kicked in the belly;
by the humiliation of the wrongly punished;
by the virgin stripped and sold,
and the son whose mother is insulted:
    I salute you, Mary.

Crown of Thorns

By the beggar whose only crown is hornets circling
in the yellow orchard, whose only scepter
a stick to drive away dogs; by the poet
whose brow bleeds in the bramble
of desires he never attains:
    I salute you, Mary.

Bearing the Cross

By the old woman stumbling under a load
too heavy, crying "oh God!"; by the unfortunate
with no human love to lean on—
as His Cross leaned on Simon of Cyrene;

137

by the horse crushed beneath his wagon:
    I salute you, Mary.

Crucifixion

By the four directions that crucify this world,
by those whose flesh is broken and fails,
by those with no feet and those with no hands,
the invalid moaning in surgery,
the innocent convicted of murder:
    I salute you, Mary.

Resurrection

By the night that passes — revealing once again
the wild rose laughing on the heart of dawn;
by the Easter bells flying wildly
on holy Saturday, flooding the valley
with halleluiahs:
    I salute you, Mary.

Ascension

By the hermit's steep climb to the summit
where white partridges roost;
by the sheep that scale the morning
to feed on honeyed snow,
and the glorious Sun rising:
    I salute you, Mary.

Pentecost

By the shepherd fires that light
the faces of the hills—those praying apostles;
the flames that cook the dark supper of the poor;
the lightning that strikes the void of every human
being
like thatch, but for Eternity:
    I salute you, Mary.

Assumption

By the crone lugging her bundle of wood to the crest
of the road and the shadow of the Cross,
whose kind son helps through her suffering;
by the dove whose flight to illumination
melts in pure prayer:
    I salute you, Mary.

Coronation of the Holy Virgin

By the Queen whose only Crown has always been
the stars—treasure of ineffable Charity,
whose only scepter, an old garden lily;
by the virgin leaning over, wreathed in the roses
of desire her love will attain:
    I salute you, Mary.

III. The Purifying Spring

J'allais chez Monsieur Lay l'instituteur

J'allais chez Monsieur Lay l'instituteur.
Mon alphabet était comme des fleurs.
Je me souviens du poêle et de la bûche
que chaque enfant du village apportait
lorsque le ciel est une blanche ruche
et qu'au réveil on dit: « Il a neigé! »

Je me souviens aussi de la gaîté
de mon tablier, aux jours mûrs d'Été,
quand je quittais l'école un peu plus tôt.
Petit à petit j'avais encor les Cieux
dedans les yeux comme une goutte d'eau
à travers quoi l'on peut voir le Bon Dieu.

Je découvrais la Terre à chaque pas.
Et voici l'eau où l'on ne marche pas,
l'air et le feu que l'on ne touche point;
et, souhaités autant qu'inabordables,
les animaux qui sont toujours plus loin
comme des rois sont pour les misérables.

O rossignol ! Oh ! Combien j'ai souffert
que tu préférasses un rosier vert
à mon cœur. Et toi, luisant capricorne,
pourquoi ne quittais-tu pas la forêt
pour t'en venir, ronflant aux moissons mornes,
vers le désir de mes petits doigts frais?

Seigneur, il y a plus de trente-quatre ans.
Et, déjà vous refusiez à l'enfant
de transformer son cœur aimable en nid
et puis encor de faire de sa main
un blanc calice où l'insecte ravi
eût bu l'eau ronde où tremble le matin.

Et maintenant, Seigneur, je viens encore
moi, votre fils, ainsi qu'à mon aurore,
vous demander des oiseaux pour mon cœur
et, pour mes mains, des bestioles de flamme.
« Il se fait tard déjà », ô mon Seigneur !
Seigneur, comblez le vide de mon âme !

School at Mr. Lay's

I attended school at Mr Lay's.
Alphabet letters were like flowers.
I remember the wood stove,
the log each child brought
when the sky was a white hive
and we woke up crying, "It snowed!"

I remember my gay smock
on full summer days
when I left school early.
Slowly heaven came back
in view — like a drop of water
through which I saw God.

At every step I discovered the Earth —
water we cannot walk on,
air and fire we do not touch,
animals we long for but
cannot reach — distant
as kings are from the poor.

Oh Nightingale! How I suffered
when you chose a green rosebush
over my heart. Shining Goat,
why not leave the woods with a snort
at its paltry crop — rushing
to my fresh, eager little fingers?

142

Lord, it has been thirty-four years
since you refused to turn the tender
heart of that child into a nest,
his hand into a white calyx
where some happy insect might sip
at morning's quivery pond.

Once again, I your son have come —
as I came in that early dawn —
to plead for songbirds in my heart
and fireflies in my hands.
It grows late. Please Lord,
fill the emptiness in my soul.

Qui avait jeté le jardin devant moi?

Qui avait jeté le jardin devant moi?
Qu'y faisait-on? Je ne comprenais pas.
Et, indécis, j'allais sous la tonnelle
pleine de nuit, de façon si légère
que pour le dire il me faudrait des ailes.
On y riait. On me tendait un verre.

Mais déjà, moi, j'étais comme une rose :
je me froissais, épineux et morose ;
et je pleurais dans tout cet infini.
Et c'est alors qu'entre toutes bénie,
sur son grand coeur solide comme un buis,
me consolait la mère de ma vie.

Dès lors, sachant ce que c'est une mère,
je m'attristais aux lis du presbytère.
Dans leur parfum il y avait un nid.
Et le curé, en tenant son bréviaire,
m'y amenait quand approchait la nuit,
disant : « Les petits dorment sous la mère. »

J'apprenais donc, mystère après mystère,
toute la vie. Au champ de la rivière
j'étais certain que, pour varier les fleurs,
tout simplement, quand on n'était pas là,
l'ange changeait les tiges, les couleurs.
Quel grand savant ne rirait de cela?

The Garden

Who cast the garden before me?
How did it happen? Confused,
unsure, I stepped under the bower
flowing with night, so lightly
I would need wings to show you.
They laughed and held out a drink.

Then I cumpled like a rose,
thorny and morose —
and I wept in all that infinity.
But the blessed mother of my life
pulled me toward her big heart —
solid as boxwood — and consoled me.

Now that I knew what a mother was,
I felt sad by the rectory lilies.
In their perfume, was a nest.
The vicar, holding his prayerbook,
took me there at night. "They are sleeping,"
he explained, "with their mother."

And so, mystery by mystery
I learned about life. I was sure
it was an angel who changed the flowers
on the river meadow for variety
when no one was looking.
A great thinker would have laughed!

Par un Dimanche qui était comme un gâteau

Par un Dimanche qui était comme un gâteau,
on me mena chez le père Fiteau,
notaire habitant en pleine campagne.
Le déjeuner était comme une fête :
lourd, triste et beau. Et j'avais pour compagne
une petite enfant qui était « la nièce ».

Et elle et moi ensuite nous allâmes
dans le verger où, ainsi que des flammes,
montaient les poiriers mélancoliques.
Les oiseax étaient confiants sur les branches.
Mon coeur, mon coeur, ce jour si magnifique
était peut-être un amour chez les anges.

A Sunday

There was a Sunday like a cake.
We had gone to the house of papa
Fiteau, the country notary.
The meal was festive—heavy,
somber and lovely. My companion,
a child called "your niece."

Afterward, she and I walked
in the orchard among the flaming,
melancholy pear trees.
Birds whispered in the branches.
Heart, oh my heart, that glorious day
was surely love among the angels.

Le pharmacien était monsieur Fourcade

Le pharmacien était monsieur Fourcade.
Il me soignait lorsque j'étais malade,
et il coiffait une perruque rousse
sous un chapeau de feutre à la Murger.
Il avait dû, étudiant à Toulouse,
aimer Mimi Pinson et les vieux airs.

Sur le coteau, sous l'émail des montagnes,
Monsieur Fourcade avait une cabane
qu'il avait baptisée: Le Paradis.
Et le fait est qu'en haut du sentier clair,
près de l'azur terrestre on aurait dit
qu'un séraphin l'avait bâtie en l'air.

Au pied du Paradis, des marjolaines
croissaient. Suave et poivrée leur haleine
grisait les pics dessinés dans les cieux.
Le pharmacien récoltait de ces fleurs
pour composer, comme un religieux,
une excellente et cordiale liqueur.

Il encageait des rats et des vipères.
Quand il venait chez la propriétaire
il lui disait: « Ah! Madame Mailou!
« Vous êtes une femme de devoir...
« Votre cochon est propre comme un sou.
« Vous devriez lui donner un miroir! »

148

The Pharmacist

The pharmacist, Mr. Fourcade,
cared for me when I was sick.
Under his felt hat, he wore a red wig.
Studying in Toulouse, he must
have loved Mimi Pinson—the songs
of the old days.

On a hill under the glazed peaks,
Mr. Fourcade had a cabin
he had christened *Paradise*.
Atop the bright path in terrestrial azure,
it did seem built in the air
by a seraphim.

Below Paradise, bloomed marjoram
that intoxicated the lofty peaks
with its soft peppery breath.
The pharmacist gathered flowers
like a monk, to create
a fine sweet liqueur.

Rats and vipers he trapped.
Visiting his landlady, he exclaimed,
"Madame Mailou, what
a dutiful woman! Your pig
is perfect as a new penny—
all he needs is a mirror!"

Quand on dînait, la face de mon père

Quand on dînait, la face de mon père
se dessinait en courbe de lumière,
brillante et fine comme un fil de rosée,
dans l'ombre de sa barbe de grand chef.
Il était ironique avec fierté,
rêveur, nerveux, beau, susceptible et bref.

Dedans son cœur peut-être, écoutait-il,
comme on écoute au creux d'une coquille,
les mornes voix des soleils des Antilles;
et, sur mon âme, voyait-il des lueurs
de colibris sur des jardins tranquilles
passer comme des éclairs de chaleur?…

Il était adroit et très patient.
Quand le Bureau de l'Enregistrement
était fermé, on pêchait à la ligne.
L'eau était verte au calme et, au courant,
ne l'était pas – mais avait l'air de rire.
« Ça mord…J'ai pris encore un poisson blanc ! »

Eau, feuillage, air, sable, racines, fleurs,
sauterelles, lombrics, martins-pêcheurs,
brume tombant sur quelque champ de raves,
grilles de vigne au toit du tisserand :
ô doux génies qui m'avez fait esclave!
Vous m'amusiez, moi, petit, vous si grands!

My Father's Face

When we dined, my father's face,
in the shadow of that commanding
beard, shone with an aura
bright and fine as a drop of dew.
He was a dreamer—ironic and proud,
strong, handsome, sensitive and taciturn.

Perhaps he could hear, inside his heart,
like the interior of a shell, mournful
voices from the sunny Antilles,
maybe he saw on my soul
hummingbirds flashing like summer
lightning over quiet gardens.

He was skilled and patient.
When the registrar's office closed,
we went fishing. The water
was either green and calm
or flowing and laughing.
"Got a bite—another white fish!"

Water, leaves, air, sand, roots,
flowers, grasshoppers, mushrooms,
kingfishers, fog over a field of beets,
vines over the weaver's roof. Sweet genies!
You enslaved, you entertained me.
I, so small, and you—so big!

151

Certes, j'étais ému par la nature

Certes, j'étais ému par la nature.
Ce cher père, enfoui dans la verdure,
ouvrait pour moi l'ineffable rideau.
Oh! cette odeur! quand il coupait des branches
pour mieux jeter sa ligne sur les eaux
oh! cette odeur de ma neuve existence!

Mais il était une autre joie plus sûre.
C'était, c'était, au crépuscule mûr,
la procession dans le cimetière.
Que je vous ressentais, ô mon Seigneur!
dans la douceur des lis, lorsque ma mère
priait tout haut et qu'en mourait mon cœur.

Ceci était plus doux que tout le reste,
que le feu bleu des insectes célestes
dont s'enflammaient et se courbaient les tiges,
plus doux que mon goûter dans le pré chaud,
plus doux que tout, plus doux que tout, vous dis-je:
car la prière est la sœur des oiseaux.

152

Moved by Nature

Certainly, I was moved by Nature.
My dear father, ensconced in green,
opened the ineffable curtain.
Oh that smell—when he cut branches
to cast his line farther over the water.
That smell of my new existence!

But there was another joy
more certain still. Our sunset
processions through the cemetery.
How I sensed you, my Lord, in the sweetness
of the lilies when my mother prayed outloud
and my heart fainted.

That was sweeter than anything else!
Than the blue fire of celestial insects
lighting, bending the stems;
than picnics on the warm meadow,
sweeter than anything, than anything, I say.
For prayer is the sister of the birds.

Je me souviens d'une procession

Je me souviens d'une procession
entre autres, en temps d'inondation,
et qui eut lieu, le soir, après dîner.
Elle chanta jusque hors de la ville.
Depuis plusieurs jours les champs et les prés
n'étaient plus que des flaques immobiles.

Mon coeur, mon coeur, ô mon coeur! Souviens-t'en.
J'avais alors un tablier et quatre ans.
Je m'inquiétais de ne pas voir ma mère.
Auprès du pont, c'était-il des tilleuls?
Les eaux noyaient les choses coutumières
qui se taisaient comme des gens en deuil.

Je me souviens de l'arbre de Saint-Jean.
On y mettait le feu, la nuit tombante.
Il devenait comme une averse d'or.
Que c'était beau! Je suis prêt à pleurer.
O Dieu du feu, je t'aime et je t'adore,
O Dieu des eaux qui priaient sur les prés!

Ecoute-moi, mon Dieu, écoute moi...
Au nom des jours lointains, au nom des mois
et des années : exauce ma prière !
O Créancier ! Cherche parmi tes coffres
ce feu de joie de l'enfance première.
Il est à toi. C'est à toi que je l'offre.

154

Louez mon Dieu ainsi que dans les Landes,
soirs parfumés comme des reines-Claude,
ô soirs de la Saint-Jean sur les coteaux !...
Quand, un à un et un à un, les feux
vont s'éteignant en ronde et que bientôt,
à l'horizon, il n'y a plus que Dieu.

One Procession in Particular

I remember one procession in particular
during the floods, that took
place in the evening after supper
and carolled to the outskirts of town.
For days, the fields and meadows
were nothing but motionless pools.

My heart, my heart, oh my heart — remember!
I was four and wore a smock.
I couldn't see Mother and was scared.
By the bridge, were those lindens?
Everything was underwater,
silent as people in mourning.

I remember the Midsummer tree.
At nightfall it was set on fire —
and became a downpour of gold.
So beautiful it was, I could weep!
God of fire, I love and adore you,
God of water that prays on the meadows.

Listen, my God, listen to me
in the name of those days, months
and years long past, hear my prayer!
Creditor, search your coffers
for that first childhood bonfire —
it is yours — and to you I offer it.

Praise God the way Landes people do—
on nights that smell of Queen Claude plums,
midsummer nights on hills where
a circle of fires slowly goes out
and finally—on the horizon—
there is nothing but God.

Après souper nous allions souvent voir

Après souper nous allions souvent voir
le vieux notaire, à son seuil nous asseoir.
Il s'appelait Monsieur Denagiscarde,
et faisait un dieu d'un avoir subtil
du patron qui, dans une Etude, à Tarbes,
lui avait appris le Code civil.

La nuit tombait, les voix faisaient silence.
On n'entendait dans la douceur immense
que le ronflement de mon cascaret.
C'était une noix formée en crécelle,
et le grillon, son frère, répondait
de la cuisine, avec sa note grêle !

N'était-ce là une belle oraison
que celle d'une noix et d'un grillon ?
Moi j'écoutais. J'écoutais sans comprendre.
Et ce murmure enveloppé par l'ombre
allait à Dieu, l'invitant à descendre
et à s'asseoir auprès des choses sombres.

After Supper

After supper, we often went to see
the old notary and sit on his porch —
Mr. Denagiscarde who deified
that subtle thing — the civil code —
his boss had taught him
in an office in Tarbes.

The night fell, our voices fell silent.
In that immense sweetness, all we heard
was my little hummer — a rattle
made from a nut — and his brother,
a cricket whose piercing reply
came from the kitchen.

A beautiful oration,
that of cricket and nut.
I listened uncomprehending
as murmurs enveloped in night
rose toward God, inviting him to descend
and join the world of darkness.

La mère de ma mère était très sainte

La mère de ma mère était très sainte.
Je la revois toujours en noir, et ceinte
d'une lueur de sereine bonté.
Elle disait, le soir, son chapelet,
et conservait la douce dignité
de ceux que Dieu a déjà appelés.

Haute, le nez busqué et les yeux verts.
Sa bouche se serrait d'un pli amer
quand on choquait sa charité chrétienne.
Je lui ai vu parfois ce très grand air;
on sentait alors quelle était sa peine,
mais qu'elle préférait ne pas parler.

Elle était comme un camée qu'elle avait:
sur son cœur net elle se profilait
et ses cheveux sur son âme neigeaient.
Dans un sac noir, elle apportait, riante,
à ses petits-enfants, qui s'empressaient,
de la réglisse et du sucre à la menthe.

Mother's Mother

Mother's mother was very holy.
I always see her dressed in black
with a halo of serene goodness.
In the evening she prayed the rosary
with the sweet dignity of those
whom God has already called.

Tall with arched nose
and green eyes, mouth closed
in a bitter tuck at any offense
to her Christian charity—sometimes
I noticed a superior air and felt her pain,
but she preferred not to speak.

She was like the cameo she wore—
carved profile over a pure heart,
hair snowing upon her soul.
Grand-children ran toward her as she
laughed and drew from her back purse
licorice and sweet mints.

Il y avait un grenier où j'allais

Il y avait un grenier où j'allais.
Là, sans savoir pourquoi, je contemplais
ce mur qui muet me rendait muet:
cette montagne où se brisait le ciel.
A l'horizon qu'est-ce que l'on trouvait?
On trouvait Dieu, les champs et le soleil.

Oui, je savais que Dieu vivait là-bas.
Il m'arrivait de faire quelques pas
—tant j'étais sûr qu'était là sa demeure—
afin d'aller le voir et lui parler.
Avais-je tort de l'y croire? À cette heure
il veille encore sur la verte vallée.

Il cueille encore, aux soirs d'août, l'origan
qui sent si bon et rime à ouragan.
Il est le Roi des petites rainettes,
et c'est par lui que marchent les nuages,
et que l'enfant regarde à la fenêtre,
et que le monde est comme des images.

The Attic

There was an attic where I went —
without knowing why — to contemplate
the silent, and silencing, wall
of the mountain — shattering the sky!
On the horizon, what did I find?
I found God, the fields and the sun.

Yes, I knew God lived there.
I would take several steps — to see
and speak to him — I was so sure
he was there. Was I imagining it?
At that hour, he still watches
over the green valley.

August evenings, he gathers sweet
marjoram that rhymes with storm.
He is the king of little frogs.
Because of him, the clouds go by,
a child looks out the window
and the world is in pictures.

Non loin de Pau, il était à Bilhères

Non loin de Pau, il était, à Bilhères,
une pelouse éblouie. La lumière
la criblait. Un dimanche, après-midi,
que je me promenais avec les bonnes,
je vis, plus beau que la beauté, je vis
un papillon dentelé, bleu, noir, jaune.

Je l'attrapai. Ce me fut un bonheur,
un tel bonheur qu'encor je suis songeur,
me demandant comment ma petite âme
put à ce point me le faire éprouver.
Le papillon était comme la flamme
des boutons d'or dont le vernis criait.

C'est tout auprès de la même prairie,
trente-trois ans plus tard, qu'anéantis
par la douleur qui fut plus grande encore
que cette joie du papillon capté,
c'est là que moi et la fauve Mamore
un jour de pluie nous nous sommes quittés.

Not Far from Pau

Not far from Pau at Bilhères,
there was a dazzling lawn—riddled
with light. One Sunday afternoon
strolling with the maids, I saw—
lovelier than loveliness itself—
a lacy butterfly, blue, black and yellow.

I caught it—and this made me
so happy that I still dream about it,
amazed my little soul could
make me feel such happiness.
The butterfly was like a flaming
buttercup shouting its brilliance.

By that same meadow,
thirty-three years later, crushed
by a grief greater even than that joy
over catching a butterfly—on a dark
rainy day—I and my wild
Mamore parted forever.

165

Vers mes cinq ans, on partit de Tournay

Vers mes cinq ans, on partit de Tournay.
Je quittai l'école de Monsieur Lay.
On vint s'installer quelques mois à Pau.
La nouvelle école était dirigée
par les deux demoiselles Letourneau
dont l'une est morte extrêmement âgée.

Elles avaient (c'était comme un secret),
appris à lire au maréchal Bosquet.
On venait là me chercher vers cinq heures.
Et, tenant un filet à papillons,
je me soûlais de l'ardente lueur
qu'a le ciel bleu quand on sort de pension.

Ah! depuis lors, j'ai mêlé mes souffrances
aux souvenirs de cette heureuse enfance.
Car, là encor, j'ai mêlé mes passions
à ces grands jours de lumière profonde
où l'écaille d'argent des papillons
choit de l'azur qui tremble comme l'onde.

Almost Five

When I was almost five,
we left Tournay and I, Mr. Lay's school.
We moved to Pau for a few months.
The new school directors were
the Letourneau sisters — one of whom
lived to a great age.

They had — in secret — taught
Marshall Bosquet how to read.
I was fetched at five o'clock.
And stepping out, butterfly net
in hand, I drank in the warm light
of the blue sky.

Since then, I have mixed sorrow
with memories of happy childhood —
as I mixed my passions then
with glories of deep light,
when silvery butterflies fell
through pulsing waves of azure.

Je me souviens de quand on allait voir

Je me souviens de quand on allait voir,
à Orthez, les grand'tantes vêtues de noir
qui avaient nom Clémence et Célanire.
Elles étaient huguenotes. Clémence,
je la revois sur les parquets qui luisent,
haute, maigre, silencieuse, glissante.

Je demandais: « Dis-moi, tante Clémence,
« Si telle chose est vraie, ou Si l'on ment? »
Elle disait: « oui – ou non – mon enfant. »
Il y avait, autour d'elle, de l'ombre,
l'ombre, je crois, de l'ancien Testament,
l'ombre de la Création du Monde.

Elle est morte à la lecture des Psaumes,
disant adieu aux épais toits de chaume,
aux fumées bleues des midis dans le ciel.
…« Car, s'il est excellent, prononça-t-elle,
de s'en aller au sein de l'Eternel :
cette heure où je vous quitte est bien cruelle ».

To Orthez

I remember going to Orthez
to visit our great-aunts Clémence
and Célanire, who wore black
and were Huguenots. I still see
Clémence, tall, thin, silent,
gliding on the shining parquet.

"Aunt Clémence," I asked,
"is it true, or is it a lie?" She answered
"Yes" or "No, my child."
There was a shadow around her —
the shadow of the Old Testament, I think,
shadow of the Creation of the World.

She died during a reading of the psalms,
saying Adieu to thick thatched roofs
and smoky blue afternoons.
"Though it is good to return
to the bosom of the Eternal," she said,
"this parting is very cruel."

C'est Dieu que j'invoquais sur my flûte rustique

C'est Dieu que j'invoquais sur my flûte rustique.
Il est venu par le doux chemin villageois,
Ainsi qu'un laboureur, tout au long d'un pavois
De campanule et d'angélique.

Il est venu par le blé mûr des catholiques.
Les perdrix, les enfants rappelaient à la fois.
Les joubarbes faisaient aux descentes des toits
Des sculptures de basilique.

Au-dessus des fronts ceints de neige et de douceur
On lisait tout en or sur la pauvre bannière :
« O mon fils ! donne-moi ton coeur ! »

Et, voyant ruisseler ces mots dans la lumiére,
Je répondais, comme en silence font les fleurs :
« Donnez-moi votre coeur, ô Père ! »

170

It Is God I Invoked

It was God I invoked on my rustic flute.
Down the quaint village road he came
like a worker — passing festive displays
    of campanula and angelica.

Through the ripe wheat of the Catholics
he came — while children and partridges
cried in unison; and succulents
    sculpted basilicas on the rooftops.

Over walls haloed in snow and sweetness,
on a tattered banner stood in gold:
    Oh son, give me your heart!

And seeing those words streaming in the light,
I answered, like the flowers, in silence:
    Give me your heart, oh Father!

Jamais ni la bruyère en feu, ni les cigales

Jamais ni la bruyère en feu, ni les cigales,
Ni la fièvre qui fait délirer un enfant,
Ni la route sans peupliers au soleil blanc,
Ni la joue amoureuse où la honte s'étale;

Ni le rosier baigné par une aube automnale,
Ni l'azure que l'on boit au puits en frissonnant,
Ni la brise à minuit qui tout à coup surprend
Le dormeur qui rêvait aux collines natales...

Jamais cette chaleur, jamais cette fraîcheur
N'atteignirent le frais ou le chaud de mon coeur
Qui croyait inventer l'amour sur cette terre,

Posséder du Printemps, de l'Eté, les primeur,
Mais reculer toujours l'Automne qui tempère
L'homme qui semble triste et qui sait le bonheur.

Blazing Moor

Neither the blazing moor nor the locust,
the fever that makes a child delirious
nor the road with no trees in white sunlight,
nor a lover's cheek red with shame;

nor the rose bathed in autumn sunrise,
nor freezing blue water drunk from the well,
nor midnight's breeze waking the sleeper
from his dream of native hills.

Neither that warmth, nor that coolness
was ever as cool or as warm as my heart was
believing it could create love on earth,

possess spring and summer fruit
and postpone forever autumn—that tempers
the man who seems sad and yet experiences joy.

La Boue sacrée

Je connais le mystère
De ton génie, ô cœur!
Une motte de terre
Mêlée avec des pleurs.

Holy Mud

I know now, oh Heart,
the secret of your genius—

a clod of earth mixed
with tears.

Le Génie

Des noms sont exaltés un à un qui s'effacent,
Tels que des flots ailés repris par l'océan;
Mais un vrai nom résiste à la mode qui passe:
Il demeure immobile au milieu du néant.

Genius

Names are exalted and expunged
one by one—like high-flying waves
swallowed by the sea.

A name that is real resists
passing fashion—in the middle
of the void unmoved.

Nuit de printemps

Ce sont des signes, mais quels signes dans les cieux?
Quand donc comprendrons-nous ce langage de Dieu
Dans cette inextricable et vaste fourmilière
De triangles tracés par des points de lumière?
Jamais je ne me suis senti plus isolé
Que lorsque vers ce bleu des nuits, taché de lait,
J'élevais mon regard sans que rien, sur la terre,
Que mon esprit quittait, me servît de repère.
Encor plus effrayant que celui de Colomb,
Quel est donc cet atlas d'or et de vermillon
Avec cet océan où la terre s'engage?
Nous savons que viendra le jour du grand naufrage.
En attendant faisons comme le rossignol
Qui sur la cime où tout finit dresse le col
Pour que le Paradis puisse à loisir entendre
Son chant nu, solitaire, anxieux, triste et tendre.

178

Spring Night

There are signs in the heavens — but what kind?
Will we ever understand the language of God
in this vast and tangled ant-heap —
these triangles traced through points of light?
Never do I feel more alone than when I raise my eyes
to night's milky blue and find none of Earth's
familiar landmarks. What is this gold and vermilion
Atlas — more frightening than Columbus had —
with its ocean the Earth must navigate?
We know the great shipwreck is coming.
While we wait, let us do as the nightingale
atop the tree where it all ends — stretching his neck
so Paradise may enjoy at leisure his naked,
solitary, anxious, sad and tender song.

La Vierge de la cathédrale Saint-André

Quand sur Bordeaux tombe l'averse à flots serrés
Qui reflète la rue, entrons à Saint-André.
La nuit et les piliers et la nef s'y confondent,
Mais tous ceux-là qu'étreint une angoisse profonde
N'hésitent point, vont droit à la Mère de Dieu.
Dans cette ombre cousue avec des points de feu,
Elle attend calme et belle, immaculée et forte,
Ses enfants bien-aimés, souffrants de mille sortes.
L'ouvrière a posé son parapluie au coin
De sa chaise, et couvert sa face de ses mains.
Enfant, est-ce un remords ou bien quelque autre peine
Qui te pousse à venir ici? Jamais la Reine
Du peuple ne repousse un calice de pleurs.
Et toi, le vieux monsieur, chauve et noir, dont le cœur
Est ridé par l'affront ou par la solitude,
Elle te versera de sa béatitude.
Et toi pauvresse, aux reins endoloris, crois-tu
Qu'elle soit insensible à tes humbles vertus?
D'ici, les pèlerins de ce monde qui passe
Ressortent allégés des maux de leur besace.

Virgin of Saint Andrew's

When heavy rains flood Bordeaux and the roads
become mirrors, let us step inside Saint Andrew's
where night and pillar and nave are one.
In the clutch of deep anguish, we go straight
to the Mother of God. In that darkness
needle-pointed with light, She waits—
calm and beautiful, pure and strong—for her
beloved children, who suffer so many maladies.
A laborer places her umbrella against a chair
covering her face with her hands.
Has remorse, child, or some other pain
driven you here? The people's Queen
never refuses a cup of tears. And you,
old gentleman bald and swarthy, your heart
shriveled from insult or loneliness—into you
She will pour her blessing. And you,
destitute woman with aching back—do you think
She could ignore your humble virtues?
The pilgrims of this passing world are
relieved of their burdens here.

La Grotte de Lourdes

La campanule est une corolle céleste
Qui jamais par les jours les plus calmes ne reste
Immobile, elle encense éternellement Dieu.
Ainsi, toi, Bernadette, au roc miraculeux
Un souffle, si léger que rien, fait battre encore
Ton cœur devant la Vierge apparue en Bigorre.
Ce roc, parce qu'un jour, telle la fleur des champs,
Tu t'y fixas, attire à lui cet océan
Que les pleurs ont formé sans cesse sur la terre.
Et ni les ex-votos suspendus à la pierre,
Ni les cierges pareils à des buissons ardents,
Ni les processions ne me touchent autant
Que cette fleur, que cette campanule, dis-je,
Que l'haleine de l'eau fait prier sur sa tige.

Lourdes Grotto

Campanula is a heavenly flower
that never rests, even on the calmest days
waving its incense before God.
Like you, Bernadette, by the miraculous rock
where the Virgin of Bigorre appeared
and the faintest breeze shook your heart.
That rock where you attached yourself
like a wildflower, drawn to the ocean of tears
that constantly pour from the earth.
And neither the ex-votos hanging there,
nor the candles burning like bushes,
nor the parades move me like this flower,
Campanula, forever praying
on its stem in the mist.

La Prière du poète

Comme un grand verre peint d'insectes et de fleurs,
Mon Dieu remplissez-moi de cette eau de candeur
Qui coule au pied du pic, des neiges élancée
Ainsi que dans le vent court une fiancée.
Je suis ivre de soif. Solitude, ô tilleul,
Oiseau qui dans la nuit chante un chant triste, seul,
Venez me disposer à recevoir la grâce.
Gitane aux pieds meurtris, mon âme est aussi lasse.
Comme le roi David, Dieu, j'ai crié vers Vous.
Donnez-moi de cette eau que je boive à genoux.
Que la forêt se taise! O silence, silence,
Voici cette fraîcheur et cette transparence.
L'eau monte, elle n'est plus maintenant que du ciel
Et qui n'efface point, sur les parois du verre,
Les insectes et fleurs que je vous offre, ô Père.

Poet's Prayer

Like a large glass painted with insects and flowers,
fill me, oh my God, with the waters of candor
that flow down the mountain to the foothills,
gushing from the snow like a fiancée
running through the wind. Oh solitude!
I am drunk with thirst! The linden bird sings
his sad lonely song through the night.
Come, prepare me for your grace.
My soul is weary as a gypsy with bruised feet.
Like King David, I have cried, oh my God.
Give me water I can drink on my knees.
Forest be still! Oh silence, silence....
Here is that freshness, transparency.
The water rises — there is only clear sky now.
And the insects, the flowers I offer are not
erased from the glass, oh Father.

Un beau midi

Un beau midi, lorsque s'envolera
Vers Dieu mon âme et quand s'effeuillera
L'angélus clair et bleu comme un lilas:
Qu'une vapeur, ô ma source Ursuya,
Comme un encens léger monte de toi;
Qu'elle obéisse à la brise qui va
Vers ma maison natale, et sur mon toit
Tombant en pluie avec sa fraîche voix.
Qu'elle accompagne un moment d'ici-bas
Au ciel mon chant qui te célébrera.

Lovely Noon

One lovely noon, when my soul flies away
to God and the angelus sets loose its petals,
clear and blue as a lilac — may a vapor —
a faint incense — rise from you,
oh my spring of Ursuya,
and follow the breeze to the house
of my birth, dropping its fresh voice
in rain on my roof — accompanying
for one earthly moment — to heaven —
my song celebrating you.

La source qui filtre

La roche, goutte
A goutte, toute
Pleine de fleurs
Dans la verdeur,
Verse son cœur.
Je vois, j'écoute
Son ruisselis
Sur l'éboulis
Bordant la route.
C'est par milliers
Qu'on voit briller
Au schiste en loques
Les pendeloques
Du lustre d'eau
Qui vite passent
Et que remplacent
Tout aussitôt
Leurs sœurs de glace.
Il pleut, il pleut.
Et, par secousses,
La fleur s'émeut
Avec la mousse.
Il pleut, il pleut
De façon douce
Sous le ciel bleu.

Purifying Spring

Drop
by drop
the rock, full
of flowers and leaves,
pours out its heart.
I see, I hear
it streaming
over rocky debris
along the road.
Thousands
of pendants
of sparkling water
dazzle on broken shale
and quickly pass,
instantly replaced
by their sisters of ice.
It rains, it rains.
And with each pelting
the flower moves
with the moss.
So gently it rains,
it rains under
the azure.

Acknowledgements

Some of these translations were previously published in *Francis Jammes: On the Life & Work of a 20th Century Master,* edited by Kathryn Nürnberger and Bruce Whiteman (Pleiades Press, University of Central Missouri, 2014); *Gratitude Prayers: Prayers, Poems & Prose for Everyday Thankfulness,* edited by June Cotner (Andrews McMeel Publishing, Kansas City, 2013), *Changing Woman* by Janine Canan (Scars Publications, Chicago, 2000); as well as the journals *Exquisite Corpse, Synchronized Chaos,* and *Tight.*

The translator warmly thanks Littlefox publisher and author Christine Mathieu in Australia for her bountiful assistance and encouragement; Nicholas and Mireille-Jammes Newman in Belgium, directors of Association Francis Jammes in France, for their invaluable contributions; and Joan Halperin, French Professor Emeritus at Saint Mary's College in California, for her helpful suggestions.

By Janine Canan

Poetry
Mystic Bliss
Ardor: Poems of Life
In the Palace of Creation: Selected Works 1969—1999
Changing Woman
Her Magnificent Body: New & Selected Poems
Shapes of Self
Of Your Seed

Poetry Translations
Star in My Forehead: Selected Poems by Else Lasker-Schüler

Stories
Journeys with Justine
Walk Now in Beauty: The Legend of Changing Woman

Essays
Goddesses, Goddesses: Essays by Janine Canan

Edited Collections
Garland of Love: 108 Sayings by Amma
Messages from Amma: In the Language of the Heart
The Rhyme of the Aged Mariness: Last Poems of Lynn Lonidier

She Rises like the Sun: Invocations of the Goddess by Contemporary American Women Poets

About Janine Canan

Janine Canan lives in California, at the foot of an extinct volcano in the Valley of the Moon. She first met Francis Jammes as a French major at Stanford University, where she graduated "with distinction." Later she attended New York University School of Medicine, and for several decades has been a practicing psychiatrist. She is a passionate feminist and a devoted student of the Indian humanitarian Mata Amritanandamayi. Janine is the award-winning author of m any books including *Mystic Bliss* and *Ardor: Poems of Life*; *Goddesses Goddesses,* a collection of essays; *Journeys with Justine,* a volume of stories; *Star in My Forehead,* a translation of the German-Jewish poet Else Lasker-Schüler; and anthologies including *Messages from Amma* and *She Rises like the Sun.*

Visit JanineCanan.com for more information.

Praise for *Under the Azure*

The poetry of Francis Jammes is one of the spiritual glories not only of the French language but of world literature. Grounded in the holy particulars of place and in the subtle miracles of ordinary life, its universal and cosmic embrace of the Divine Feminine in nature and human and divine love sings beyond all cultural and religious boundaries. In Janine Canan's exemplary, tender and profoundly lyrical and transparent translations, it is now available to all English-speaking readers and seekers. I cannot recommend the radiance and revelation of this book enough. —*Andrew Harvey, author of Light upon Light: Inspirations from Rumi*

Francis Jammes felt deeply the sadness of being human in the bountiful beauty of nature. He made music of his sorrow and delight, a music both simple and mysterious. Francis Jammes, like his namesake Saint Francis, makes one more tender, more tolerant, more awed by what is. Janine Canan, whose poetry and sensibility drew her to Jammes, makes you hear the whoosh of the angels' wings in his poetry, a whoosh that is the same in every language, but yields only to the highest art of translation. This is a

marvelous book of poetry. —*Andrei Codrescu, author of Jealous Witness: New Poems*
No description can convey the delicate dream-power of Jammes' poems, which impressed the greatest modern French writers, including Stéphane Mallarmé, Paul Claudel and André Gide. To my knowledge, this is the first book-length selection of Jammes' work in English for over a quarter-of-a-century; many of the poems appear here in translation for the first time, carefully rendered by Janine Canan. If you don't yet know Jammes, this is a good place to encounter the naturalistic spiritual delirium of his verse: "The water mirrors the pure azure/ poised on the golden tips of the moss." Subtle and dizzying at once, Jammes can convert the most committed unbeliever. —*Justin Clemens, Readings Monthly*

Not only are Janine Canan's translations in *Under the Azure: Poems of Francis Jammes* gorgeous throughout — but she includes a forward by Jammes' granddaughter, and a great introduction that illuminates the life of Jammes, "poet of the Pyrenees." —*Katherine Hastings, Word Temple*

196

www.ingramcontent.com/pod-product-compliance
Lightning Source LLC
Chambersburg PA
CBHW060756100426
42813CB00004B/840